M000114687

P · E · R · F · E · C · T
CASSEROLES

P·E·R·F·E·C·T
CASSEROLES

DORLING KINDERSLEY
LONDON • NEW YORK • STUTTGART • MOSCOW

A DORLING KINDERSLEY BOOK

Created and Produced by
CARROLL & BROWN LIMITED
5 Lonsdale Road
London NW6 6RA

Editorial Director Jeni Wright
Editor Anna Brandenburger
Editorial Assistant Julia Alcock

Managing Art Editor Lyndel Donaldson
Art Editor Lucy De Rosa
Designer Alan Watt
Production Editor Wendy Rogers

First Published in Great Britain in 1997
by Dorling Kindersley Limited
9 Henrietta Street, London WC2E 8PS

Previously published in 1993 under the title
Look & Cook Creative Casseroles

Copyright © 1993, 1997 Dorling Kindersley Limited
Text copyright © 1993, 1997 Anne Willan Inc.

Visit us on the World Wide Web at http://www.dk.com

All rights reserved. No part of this publication may be
reproduced, stored in a retrieval system, or transmitted in
any form or by any means, electronic, mechanical, photocopying,
recording, or otherwise, without the prior written permission
of the copyright owner.

A CIP catalogue record for this book is available
from the British Library

ISBN 0-7513-0390-9

Reproduced by Colourscan, Singapore
Printed and bound in Singapore by Star Standard

CONTENTS

PERFECT CASSEROLES

Welcome to **Perfect Casseroles**. This volume is designed to be the simplest most informative cookbook you'll ever own. It is the closest I can come to sharing my personal techniques for cooking my own favourite recipes without actually being with you in the kitchen looking over your shoulder.

Equipment and ingredients often determine whether or not you can cook a particular dish, so **Perfect Casseroles** sets out everything you need at the beginning of each recipe. You'll see at a glance how long a recipe takes to cook, how many servings it makes, what the finished dish looks like, and how much preparation can be done ahead. When you start to cook, you'll find the preparation and cooking are organized into steps that are easy to follow. Each stage has its own colour coding and everything is shown in photographs with brief text to go with each step. You will never be in doubt as to what it is you are doing, why you are doing it, and how it should look.

EQUIPMENT

INGREDIENTS

🍽 SERVES 4–6   🥣 WORK TIME 25–35 MINUTES   🍲 COOKING TIME 20–30 MINUTES

I've also included helpful hints and ideas under "Anne Says". These may list an alternative ingredient or piece of equipment, or explain a certain method, or add some advice on mastering a particular technique. Similarly, if there is a crucial stage in a recipe when things can go wrong, I've included some warnings called "Take Care".

Many of the photographs are annotated to pinpoint why certain pieces of equipment work best, and how food should look at the various stages of cooking. Because presentation is so important, a picture of the finished dish with serving suggestions is at the end of each recipe.

Thanks to all this information you can't go wrong. I'll be with you every step of the way. So please come with me into the kitchen to look, cook, and enjoy some **Perfect Casseroles**.

Anne Willan

WHY CASSEROLES?

A casserole baking in the oven or a hearty stew simmering on the stove is one of the most comforting of home-cooked foods. Often cooked and served in a single pot, casseroles are the solution to today's busy lifestyle where convenience is the key and quick clean-up is mandatory. Casseroles are balanced meals in themselves, combining meat or seafood with nutritious vegetables, and often need no accompaniment except a slice of crusty bread. Whether a slow-cooked country stew or an elegant seafood chowder, there is a casserole for every cook, to suit any occasion.

RECIPE CHOICE

In this book you'll find my favourite casseroles from many countries. Hungary provides the inspiration for *Chicken Paprika with Caraway Dumplings*; *Thai Chicken and Prawns* adds a flavour of the Far East; while a *garam masala* of cumin, coriander, turmeric, and cayenne pepper gives an exotic flavour to *Indian Lamb Curry*. America is the home of *Scallop and Sweetcorn Chowder*, while from across the sea come *Irish Stew* and French *Lamb Chops Champvallon*. There are casseroles with meat, chicken, turkey, or duck, some with fish and shellfish, and some with pasta and vegetables.

SEAFOOD CASSEROLES

Monkfish and White Wine Stew: an elegant recipe, with garden vegetables and white wine. *Monkfish and Red Wine Stew:* red wine adds a robust flavour to this stew of monkfish, mushrooms, and pickling onions. *Scallop and Sweetcorn Chowder:* the sweetness of scallops and sweetcorn is paired with the salt of bacon in this American classic. *Oyster Stew with Fennel:* the anise flavour of fennel and Pernod highlights the taste of oysters in this sophisticated stew. *Prawn and Okra Gumbo:* okra gives the characteristic glutinous texture to gumbo with prawns, oysters, smoked sausage, peppers, and tomatoes. *Gumbo z'Herbes:* spicy mixed greens are mellowed by the addition of a bacon hock and sausage in this gumbo. *Paella:* prawns, mussels, sausage, and chicken are simmered with saffron rice in this quintessentially Spanish dish. *Seafood Paella:* invite family or friends to enjoy this rice dish of squid, prawns, and clams. *Five-Spice Fillet of Salmon:* salmon,

with the exotic flavour of Chinese five-spice powder, is pan-fried then baked on a bed of carrots, courgettes, and leeks. *Salmon Fillets with Mushroom and Leek Julienne:* an elegant dish of pink salmon with contrasting julienne of mushrooms and leeks. *Seafood and Tomato Stew:* a hearty stew of tomato broth packed with crabs, mussels, scallops, and white fish. *Fish Cioppino:* a variety of fish, including halibut, monkfish, and tuna, are simmered in this delicious stew.

POULTRY AND MEAT CASSEROLES

Chicken Paprika with Caraway Dumplings: from eastern Europe, this rich stew is flavoured with paprika and dotted with caraway dumplings. *Chicken and Paprika Pilaf:* rice and chicken are cooked with tomatoes, green pepper, onion, garlic, paprika, and oregano. *Chicken and Beer Stew:* chicken takes on a robust flavour, cooked in beer with juniper berries and onions. *Chicken with Cognac:* for a sophisticated dinner, chicken is simmered with pickling onions and Cognac. *Chicken in a Pot:* a whole chicken is poached in chicken stock, with aromatic vegetables, then served with sauce gribiche for a two-course meal. *Tarragon Chicken:* a classic dish of chicken in a tarragon sauce with turnips. *Turkey Mole:* in this simplified Mexican recipe, chilli powder adds heat to the rich, aromatic sauce with bittersweet chocolate. *Pork Mole:* pork chops are cooked in a spicy sauce and served with soured cream. *Poussins with Plums and Cabbage:* small whole birds are cooked *en cocotte* with shredded cabbage, bacon, and purple plums for a touch of sweetness. *Poussins with Carrots and Cabbage:* a light but satisfying country-style casserole that is ideal for winter days. *Malaysian Chicken and Prawns:* bean sprouts, coconut milk, tofu, ginger, fresh coriander, and spices give an Asian twist to chicken and prawns; thin rice noodles thicken the stew. *Thai Chicken and Prawns:* fresh hot chillies and lemon grass make the Thai version of chicken and prawns. *Duck with Turnips and Apricots:* duck is jointed and cooked with turnips, dried apricots, and Madeira for a touch of sweetness. *Duck with Fresh Figs and Port:* fresh figs contrast with the richness of duck in a port sauce. *Indian Lamb Curry:* slow cooking imparts mellow flavour to lamb, with lentils, aubergines, and cauliflower in a spicy sauce. *Indian Chicken Curry:* chicken replaces the lamb, while chickpeas add body to this spicy stew. *Lamb Chops Champvallon:* this French dish of lamb chops baked between slices of potato and onion dates back from the time of Louis XIV. *Irish Stew:* leeks take the place of onions for a contemporary update on the famous family dish. *Ham Baked with Prunes in Rich Wine Sauce:* ham is baked with prunes in a sweet-sour sauce with vinegar and caramel. *Ham with White Wine and Apples:* white wine, cream, and apples add succulence to thick slices of ham. *Beef, Barley, and Mushroom Stew:* barley adds body and character to beef and mushrooms simmered in beef stock. *Barley and Vegetable Stew:* in this stew, peas, sweetcorn, carrots, celery, and onions are cooked with barley. *Portuguese Pork and Clam Stew:* clams add zest to tender pork marinated in white wine flavoured with herbs, then slowly cooked with onions and tomatoes. *Chilean Pork and Beans:* a hearty pork stew packed with beans, peppers, tomatoes, potatoes, and herbs. *French Beef and Herb Potato Pie:* minced beef acquires French chic when combined with white wine, tomatoes, and garlic, then topped with a layer of creamy potato purée flavoured with basil and parsley. *Old Emily's Shepherd's Pie:* minced lamb is the base for this family favourite, baked in individual dishes. *Peppery Tuscan Beef Stew:* sage-flavoured *fettunta* (toasts) accompany this

rustic Italian stew of beef, tomatoes, pancetta, red wine, and garlic, with plenty of black pepper for piquancy. *Italian Beef and Rosemary Stew:* typical Italian ingredients, rosemary and olives, marry with beef and a dry white wine for a warming winter treat. *Springtime Veal Stew:* fresh fennel adds flavour and carrots give colour to the pale delicacy of veal in an ivory cream sauce that is thickened with egg yolk. *French White Veal Stew:* a classic white *blanquette* of button mushrooms and veal in a rich cream sauce. *Mock Venison Stew:* lamb shanks are transformed to resemble venison by marinating and braising in red wine with aromatic vegetables. *Venison Stew with Pears:* wedges of pear show how successful the partnership of fruit with game can be.

VEGETABLE AND PASTA CASSEROLES

Perfect Pasta and Cheese: quill-shaped pasta baked in a rich cheese sauce, embellished with both wild and common mushrooms, makes a sophisticated version of macaroni cheese. *Perfect Pasta with Three Cheeses:* green spinach pasta gives flavour and colour contrast to the rich sauce of the hard, blue-veined, and creamy French cheeses. *Roasted Pepper Lasagne with Mushrooms:* plenty of roasted red and green peppers, with mushrooms, tomato sauce, and ricotta cheese make a light and tasty lasagne. *Lasagne with Spinach:* an attractive supper dish of layers of green spinach, red tomato sauce, and white ricotta cheese– the colours of the Italian flag. *Aubergine Parmigiana:* the Italian classic of sliced aubergines layered with a rich

tomato sauce, basil, mozzarella, and freshly grated Parmesan cheese – topped with more cheese then baked until bubbling and brown. *Tian of Mediterranean Vegetables:* aubergine and courgette slices, baked with tomatoes, onions, and thyme, go into my version of a Provençal *tian*, or baked vegetable dish.

EQUIPMENT

The range of dishes is wide in this book, but the equipment needed to make them is very simple. Basic, of course, is the casserole dish itself. It should have a tight-fitting lid with a heatproof handle, though you can cover it with a double layer of foil. Enamelled cast iron is a favourite because it spreads the heat evenly and looks attractive. Other materials include stainless steel, which is easy to keep clean, but should have an aluminium or copper base, and anodyzed aluminium which is light in weight and spreads heat well.

You will also need a baking dish; the size will be stated in the recipe. You have the option of heatproof glass, china, and earthenware. Enamelled cast iron gratin dishes can also be used. Note that metal takes time to heat in the oven, so baking time may be approximate.

You will need a chef's knife for cutting up poultry and meat and for preparing large vegetables, plus a small knife for small to medium vegetables. Knives should be regularly sharpened and stored carefully so the edges remain sharp. Never soak knives or put them in the dishwasher.

In many recipes, a 2-pronged fork is used with meat and poultry during and after frying. Some recipes call for a food processor or blender, for instance to purée the sauce mixture for Turkey Mole. Others require a potato masher to make the potato purée topping.

If you are preparing a recipe that involves marinating meat, poultry, fish, or vegetables, use a non-metallic bowl so it will not react with the acid in the marinade.

INGREDIENTS

Starting with the main ingredients, seafood lovers can choose from casseroles with prawns, mussels, oysters, and scallops, or fish such as monkfish, salmon, halibut, and cod. Poultry includes a chicken simmered with vegetables, chicken pieces in a variety of tempting sauces, plus recipes for duck with fruit, and turkey in a Mexican mole sauce.

The four main meats – beef, lamb, pork, and veal – feature frequently. Often less expensive cuts can be used in a casserole, as the long slow cooking tenderizes them. When combined with hearty grains and pulses, such as barley, dried beans, and lentils, you can create a substantial meal to feed the whole family. A handful of recipes are based on pasta, including some vegetarian ideas.

Stocks – beef, veal, chicken, or fish – can be the backbone of a casserole, intensifying the flavours while providing liquid in which to cook the ingredients. Equally important is the allium family – onions, garlic, and shallots, while earthy roots such as potatoes, turnips, leeks, and carrots add substance. Leafy greens, cabbage, okra, sweetcorn, and fennel all appear in these casserole recipes. Both wild and common mushrooms play a role, as do the sun-loving vines: aubergines, tomatoes, peppers, and courgettes. Fruit is teamed with meat and poultry to add a touch of sweetness, while dried and fresh chillies, fresh root ginger, coconut milk, lemon grass, vinegar, and lemon juice add a further dimension, together with spices such as cayenne pepper, nutmeg, cinnamon, cumin, and turmeric. You'll also find familiar fresh herbs. Their fragrant leaves are either added at the beginning of cooking to blend with other ingredients or are stirred into a casserole at the last minute to impart fresh flavour and colour.

TECHNIQUES

You'll be shown many useful techniques in this book, because casseroles are so diverse. The preparation of everyday vegetables is covered: peeling, seeding, and chopping tomatoes; slicing and chopping onions, peppers, carrots, leeks, and potatoes; and shredding cabbage. You will see how to peel peppers by roasting them first, which also gives them a delicious smoky flavour. Peeling and crushing garlic is made simple with a quick blow from a heavy knife-blade. None of these techniques is difficult, and you will soon master the common ones.

In addition, you will learn how to carry out tasks as varied as trussing and jointing a chicken. There are instructions on preparing fresh root ginger by peeling, crushing, and chopping it. Cleaning and cooking mussels is explained, as well as removing the vein from prawns.

Cooking techniques are varied. Sometimes meat or poultry are browned before being simmered in a liquid, to add flavour and colour. In other recipes meat is added raw to a liquid, then cooked very gently for a long time, to soften and add richness to the sauce.

Many casseroles include a sauce. I show you how to make a cheese sauce and a rich brown roux (flour and oil mixture) to give the characteristic flavour to an American gumbo. Some sauces are lightly thickened with arrowroot. Reduction of cooking liquid is the key to good sauces, and you'll find this clearly explained too.

MONKFISH AND WHITE WINE STEW

🍽 SERVES 6   🥣 WORK TIME 45–50 MINUTES   🍲 COOKING TIME 25–30 MINUTES

EQUIPMENT

colander

large frying pan

chef's knife   paper towels

small knife   palette knife

saucepans, 1 with lid

bread knife

wooden spoon

chopping board

The delicate flavour of monkfish is highlighted with vegetables and white wine. Kneaded butter (beurre manié) gives the sauce a velvety consistency.

GETTING AHEAD

The vegetable broth can be cooked up to 8 hours ahead and kept, covered, in the refrigerator. Reheat it gently on top of the stove, then cook the fish, and finish the stew.

metric	SHOPPING LIST	imperial
750 g	skinned monkfish fillets	1½ lb
	salt and pepper	
2	shallots	2
2	garlic cloves	2
2	leeks	2
250 g	mushrooms	8 oz
1	small bunch of parsley	1
3–5	sprigs of fresh thyme	3–5
500 g	small courgettes	1 lb
75 g	butter, at room temperature	2½ oz
1	bay leaf	1
250 ml	dry white wine	8 fl oz
500 ml	fish stock (see box, page 124)	16 fl oz
45 ml	flour	3 tbsp
	For the fried croûtes	
6	slices of white bread	6
45 g	butter	1½ oz
45 ml	vegetable oil	3 tbsp

INGREDIENTS

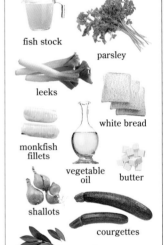

fish stock

parsley

leeks

white bread

monkfish fillets

vegetable oil

butter

shallots

courgettes

bay leaf

plain flour

garlic

thyme   white wine

mushrooms

ORDER OF WORK

1 PREPARE THE MONKFISH AND THE VEGETABLES

2 SIMMER THE BROTH; MAKE THE CROUTES

3 COOK THE FISH AND THICKEN THE STEW

1 PREPARE THE MONKFISH AND THE VEGETABLES

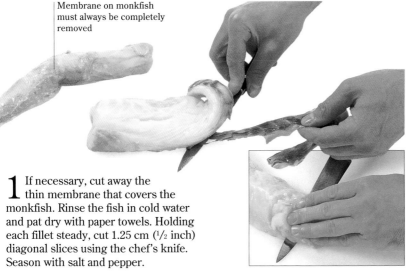

Membrane on monkfish must always be completely removed

1 If necessary, cut away the thin membrane that covers the monkfish. Rinse the fish in cold water and pat dry with paper towels. Holding each fillet steady, cut 1.25 cm (1/2 inch) diagonal slices using the chef's knife. Season with salt and pepper.

2 Peel the shallots; separate them into sections, if necessary. Slice each one horizontally, then vertically, towards the root, leaving the slices attached. Cut across into dice. Lightly crush each garlic clove. Discard the skin and finely chop the garlic.

3 Trim the leeks. With the chef's knife, slit them lengthwise, then cut them diagonally into 1.25 cm (1/2 inch) pieces.

Slit leeks before washing to open out layers

4 Wash the leeks thoroughly in the colander, under cold running water. Leave them to drain well.

5 Wipe the mushroom caps with damp paper towels and trim the stalks even with the caps. Cut the mushrooms into quarters.

7 Trim the courgettes and cut them into 5 cm (2 inch) pieces. Cut each piece lengthwise into quarters. With the small knife, cut away the seeds and trim the edges of the pieces to give a rounder shape.

Courgette pieces will form neat shapes for stew

Courgettes are trimmed into torpedo-shaped pieces

6 Strip the parsley and thyme leaves from the stalks. Pile the parsley leaves on the chopping board and finely chop them with the chef's knife.

2 SIMMER THE BROTH; MAKE THE CROUTES

1 Melt 30 g (1 oz) of the butter in a large pan, sauté the shallots, garlic, and leeks, stirring occasionally, until soft, 3–5 minutes.

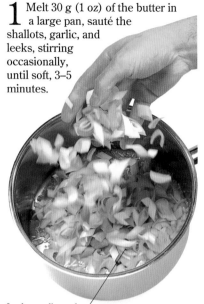

Leeks, garlic, and shallots are softened in butter to mellow flavour

2 Add the mushroom quarters, thyme, bay leaf, salt, and pepper to the saucepan, and stir to combine. Pour in the white wine and fish stock, cover the saucepan with the lid, and simmer, 10–15 minutes.

3 Add the courgettes and continue cooking until the vegetables are just tender, 8–10 minutes longer.

Fried croûtes are easily turned using palette knife

4 Meanwhile, cut the crusts from the bread, then cut each slice into 4 triangles. Melt one-third of the butter and oil in the frying pan. Add 8 bread triangles and fry until golden, 1–2 minutes. Turn the croûtes and continue frying until golden, 30–60 seconds longer. Drain on paper towels and fry the remaining croûtes in the remaining butter and oil in 2 batches.

Triangular croûtes will brown evenly when fried in batches

ANNE SAYS
"The croûtes can be prepared ahead. Wrap them in foil so they are easy to reheat in a low oven."

3 COOK THE FISH AND THICKEN THE STEW

1 Add the monkfish to the broth with water, if necessary, so that the fish is barely covered, and stir to combine.

! TAKE CARE !
Stir the stew gently so the monkfish does not fall apart.

2 Cover the pan, bring back to a boil, and simmer until the fish is tender when tested with a fork, 3–5 minutes.

3 Make the kneaded butter: using a fork, blend the remaining butter with the flour to form a smooth paste. Add the paste to the broth with your fingers. Stir to combine, so it melts into the sauce and thickens it. Simmer, 2 minutes.

Stir kneaded butter gradually into stew so it melts evenly

4 Discard the bay leaf, stir in half of the chopped parsley, and taste the stew for seasoning.

🍽 TO SERVE
Transfer the stew to a warmed tureen, sprinkle with the remaining parsley, and serve with the fried croûtes.

Monkfish retains firm texture in hearty stew

Crunchy croûtes are good contrast to velvety stew

V A R I A T I O N

MONKFISH AND RED WINE STEW

Known in French as Lotte en Meurette, *this dish commonly includes mushrooms and pickling onions in the sauce.*

1 Omit the garlic, leeks, parsley, thyme, courgettes, and white wine. Prepare the monkfish, shallots, and mushrooms as directed.
2 Make the croûtes as directed. Cook the shallots in butter until soft, 1 minute. Add 500 ml (16 fl oz) red wine; simmer until reduced by half.
3 Meanwhile, peel 250 g (8 oz) pickling onions. Melt 30 g (1 oz) butter in a frying pan, add the onions and cook until golden, 5–8 minutes. Add the mushrooms and cook until the liquid evaporates and the mushrooms are tender, 3–5 minutes.
4 Add 500 ml (16 fl oz) fish stock and 1 bay leaf to the red wine. Add the monkfish and cover. Simmer until the fish is tender, 3–5 minutes.
5 Stir in the onions and mushrooms and thicken the stew as directed. Serve on warmed individual plates.

SCALLOP AND SWEETCORN CHOWDER

🍽 SERVES 6–8 🥄 WORK TIME 25–30 MINUTES 🍲 COOKING TIME 15–20 MINUTES

EQUIPMENT

large pan

colander

paper towels

chopping board

bowls

wooden spoon

slotted spoon

chef's knife

small knife

vegetable peeler

This American classic marries the sweetness of scallops and sweetcorn with the saltiness of bacon, adding potatoes for body. You can use either large or small scallops. Oyster crackers, available from some specialist delicatessens, are the traditional accompaniment.

GETTING AHEAD

The chowder can be prepared, without the scallops, up to 1 day ahead and kept, covered, in the refrigerator. Gently reheat it on top of the stove until simmering, and cook the scallops just before serving.

metric	SHOPPING LIST	imperial
250 g	streaky bacon rashers	8 oz
2	onions	2
4	fresh corn cobs	4
500 g	new potatoes	1 lb
750 g	scallops	1½ lb
1	bay leaf	1
	salt and pepper	
750 ml	fish stock (see box, page 124)	1¼ pints
250 ml	single cream	8 fl oz
500 ml	milk	16 fl oz
	paprika for sprinkling	

INGREDIENTS

onions   bay leaf   paprika

corn cobs†   bacon

single cream   fish stock

scallops   new potatoes

milk

†300 g (10 oz) defrosted sweetcorn kernels can also be used

ANNE SAYS
"For a lighter chowder, you can substitute milk for the cream."

ORDER OF WORK

1. PREPARE THE CHOWDER INGREDIENTS

2. COOK THE CHOWDER

1 PREPARE THE CHOWDER INGREDIENTS

1 Stack the bacon rashers on the chopping board and cut them crosswise into strips about 1.25 cm (¹/₂ inch) wide, using the chef's knife.

Stacking bacon rashers makes cutting into strips quicker

2 Peel the onions with the small knife, leaving a little of the root attached. Halve and thinly slice the onions (see box, below).

3 Hold each fresh corn cob vertically on the chopping board and cut from the tip down to the board with the chef's knife. Rotate the cob and continue removing as many kernels as possible. Put the kernels in a small bowl. Working over the bowl, with the back of the knife, scrape all the pulp and milk from each corn cob.

Back of knife is best for pressing pulp from ears of corn

Sweetcorn adds golden colour to chowder

HOW TO SLICE AN ONION

*Onions are often sliced for soups and stews, as well as for sautéing.
The root is left on for slicing, to help hold the onion together.*

1 Using a chef's knife, cut the onion lengthwise in half through the root and stalk end.

2 Lay each half, cut-side down, on a chopping board, and cut across into thin or thick slices, as required.

Cut onion into slices of even thickness

4 Peel the potatoes using the vegetable peeler. With the chef's knife, cut each potato into 4–5 pieces, depending on its size.

5 If necessary, discard the tough, crescent-shaped membrane at the side of each scallop. Rinse the scallops in a bowl of cold water and drain. If using large scallops, cut each one into 2 rounds.

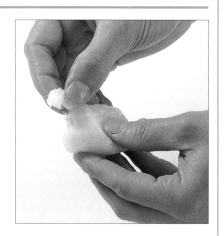

2 COOK THE CHOWDER

1 Heat the large pan, add the bacon, and fry, stirring with the wooden spoon, until the fat is rendered (melted), 3–5 minutes. With the slotted spoon, transfer the bacon to a plate lined with paper towels.

Pour in fish stock to cover potatoes generously

3 Add the potatoes to the pan with the bay leaf, salt, and pepper. Pour in the fish stock. Bring to a boil and simmer gently until the potatoes are just slightly soft when pierced with the tip of the small knife, 7–10 minutes.

After stock has been added, stir to dissolve browned juices at bottom of pan

2 Lower the heat, then add the sliced onions, and cook, stirring frequently with the wooden spoon, until soft and translucent, 3–5 minutes. With the slotted spoon, transfer the onions to the lined plate. Discard any remaining fat from the pan.

4 Return the cooked bacon and onions to the pan with the sweetcorn kernels and pulp; stir to combine.

5 Pour in the cream and milk, and stir until blended. Bring to a boil and simmer until the potatoes are tender, 7–10 minutes longer.

6 Add the scallops to the pan and stir to combine. Bring the chowder just back to simmering, then remove the pan from the heat. Discard the bay leaf, taste the chowder for seasoning, and adjust if needed.

! TAKE CARE !
Do not overcook the scallops or they will be tough; the heat of the chowder will continue to cook them after the pan has been removed from the heat.

🍽 TO SERVE
Serve the chowder in bowls, sprinkled with paprika. Accompany with oyster crackers, if you like.

Bacon contrasts with sweetness of scallops and sweetcorn

Oyster crackers are traditional accompaniment for American chowders

VARIATION

OYSTER STEW WITH FENNEL

In this American stew, oysters are paired with fennel and a dash of Pernod.

1 Omit the onions, sweetcorn, and fish stock. Substitute 32 fresh or bottled oysters (about 500 ml/16 fl oz) for the scallops, reserving the oyster juice.
2 Chop the bacon and prepare the potatoes as directed. Trim and slice 2 large fennel bulbs (total weight about 750 g/1½ lb). Strain the oyster juice into a measuring jug and add enough water to make 750 ml (1¼ pints) liquid.
3 Fry the bacon as directed until crisp, and remove it from the pan. Add the sliced fennel and cook gently, stirring occasionally, until very soft and just starting to brown, 15–20 minutes.
4 Add the potatoes, bay leaf, salt, and pepper; pour over the oyster liquid. Bring to a boil and simmer until the potatoes soften, 7–10 minutes.
5 Add half of the bacon, the cream, and milk; simmer until the potatoes are tender, 7–10 minutes longer.
6 Stir in the oysters; simmer until their edges curl, 30–60 seconds. Remove from the heat, stir in 45–60 ml (3–4 tbsp) Pernod or other anise liqueur, and taste for seasoning. Spoon the stew into 6–8 warmed bowls; sprinkle with remaining bacon.

PRAWN AND OKRA GUMBO

🍽 SERVES 8   🥄 WORK TIME 45–50 MINUTES*   ♨ COOKING TIME 1–1¼ HOURS

EQUIPMENT

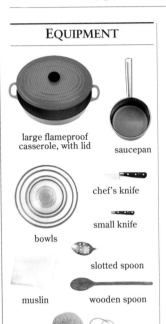

large flameproof casserole, with lid

saucepan

bowls

chef's knife

small knife

slotted spoon

muslin

wooden spoon

kitchen string

chopping board

In Louisiana, gumbo can be made from any number of ingredients. Best of all is prawn gumbo bolstered, as here, with oysters. It is thickened with a dark roux of flour toasted slowly in oil.

*plus 25–30 minutes for the roux

INGREDIENTS

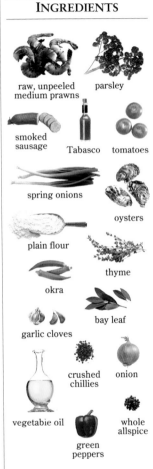

raw, unpeeled medium prawns

parsley

smoked sausage

Tabasco

tomatoes

spring onions

oysters

plain flour

thyme

okra

garlic cloves

bay leaf

vegetabie oil

crushed chillies

onion

whole allspice

green peppers

metric	SHOPPING LIST	imperial
1	large onion	1
3	garlic cloves	3
750 g	okra	1½ lb
500 g	tomatoes	1 lb
2	green peppers	2
250 g	smoked sausage, such as kielbasa	8 oz
1 kg	raw, unpeeled medium prawns	2 lb
1	bunch of parsley	1
1	small bunch of spring onions	1
	salt and pepper	
1.5 litres	water	2⅓ pints
24	shelled oysters, about 375 ml (12 fl oz)	24
2.5 ml	Tabasco sauce, more to taste	½ tsp
	For the roux	
75 ml	vegetable oil	2½ fl oz
60 g	plain flour	2 oz
	For the spice bag	
1	bay leaf	1
3–5	sprigs of fresh thyme	3–5
7.5 ml	whole allspice	1½ tsp
3.75 ml	crushed chillies	¾ tsp

ORDER OF WORK

1 PREPARE GUMBO INGREDIENTS

2 COOK THE GUMBO

1 PREPARE GUMBO INGREDIENTS

1 Peel the onion, leaving a little of the root attached; cut it lengthwise in half. Slice each half horizontally, then vertically, towards the root, leaving the slices attached at the root end. Finally, cut across to make dice.

2 Set the flat side of the chef's knife on top of each garlic clove and strike it with your fist. Discard the skin and finely chop the garlic.

Okra will give characteristic slightly glutinous texture to gumbo

3 With the chef's knife, trim the stalks and tips from the okra; cut the okra across into 1 cm (³/₈ inch) slices.

Neatly cut pieces ensure okra will cook evenly

4 Cut the cores from the tomatoes and score an "x" on the base of each. Immerse in boiling water until the skins start to split, 8–15 seconds, depending on their ripeness. Transfer at once to a bowl of cold water. When cool, peel off the skins. Cut them crosswise in half, squeeze out the seeds, then coarsely chop each half.

HOW TO PEEL AND DEVEIN PRAWNS

Prawns have a dark intestinal vein along the back that should be removed before cooking.

Shell comes off easily in your fingers

1 Peel all of the shell from each prawn with your fingers, and discard the shell.

2 Using a small knife, make a shallow cut along the back of the prawn.

3 With the help of the small knife, gently pull out the dark intestinal vein and discard it.

5 Core the peppers. Halve them and scrape out the seeds. Slice lengthwise into thin strips. Gather the strips together and cut into dice.

6 If necessary, remove the outer casing from the sausage. Using the chef's knife, cut it into 1 cm (³⁄₈ inch) slices. Peel and devein the prawns (see box, page 19).

7 Make the spice bag: combine the bay leaf, thyme, allspice, and crushed chillies; tie them up in a piece of muslin.

Muslin lets out flavour but holds in spices

8 Strip the parsley leaves from the stalks, and finely chop the leaves. Trim the stalks and tough green tops from the spring onions. Slice them crosswise on the diagonal, including some of their green tops.

2 COOK THE GUMBO

1 Make the roux: heat the oil in the casserole. Stir in the flour and cook over very low heat, stirring constantly with the wooden spoon, until the roux is medium brown, 25–30 minutes.

ANNE SAYS
"*To avoid constant stirring, cook the roux in a 230°C (450°F, Gas 8) oven 25–30 minutes. When cooked, the roux should be a dark caramel colour.*"

2 Stir the onions, garlic, peppers, salt, and pepper into the roux, and cook, stirring constantly, until they are softened and just lightly browned, 7–10 minutes. Add the tomatoes and sausage to the casserole and stir to combine. Cook, stirring occasionally, 10–12 minutes longer.

3 Add the okra, spice bag, and water. Partially cover the casserole and simmer, stirring occasionally, until the okra is very tender and the gumbo is thick and rich, 40–50 minutes.

4 Just before serving, add the prepared prawns to the gumbo and simmer gently until they begin to lose their transparency and start to turn pink, 3–5 minutes.

5 Add the oysters and spring onions; cook until the edges of the oysters start to curl, 1–2 minutes longer.

! TAKE CARE !
Do not overcook the oysters or they will be tough and chewy.

6 Remove from the heat and discard the spice bag. Stir in the parsley and Tabasco sauce. Taste for seasoning, adding more Tabasco sauce, if you like.

Hot Tabasco sauce is usual way to spice gumbo

¶❚❘ TO SERVE
Spoon the gumbo into a warmed large tureen or into individual soup bowls. Serve very hot.

Shellfish and smoked sausage are a popular Louisiana combination

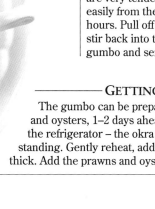

This gumbo is usually made with a variety of greens. Tradition has it that you invite as many friends as the number of greens you serve.

1 Omit the tomatoes, peppers, parsley, spring onions, prawns, and oysters. Slice the sausage and okra as directed.
2 Wash the leaves from 375 g (12 oz) each of spring greens, watercress, and 1 head of escarole (about 375 g/12 oz), discarding any tough stalks.
3 Put the wet greens in a casserole and sprinkle with salt. Cover and steam, stirring frequently, 10–12 minutes. Drain and reserve any liquid. Let cool, then roughly chop them.
4 Make the spice bag as directed, adding 3–5 sprigs of fresh oregano.
5 Make the roux; cook the onions and garlic as directed. Stir in the chopped greens, 1 smoked meaty bacon hock (about 500 g/1 lb), the sausage, okra, water, and the greens cooking liquid.
6 Cover and simmer until the greens are very tender and the meat falls easily from the bacon hock, 1¼–1½ hours. Pull off the meat, shred it, and stir back into the greens. Taste the gumbo and serve it over boiled rice.

GETTING AHEAD
The gumbo can be prepared, without the prawns and oysters, 1–2 days ahead and kept, covered, in the refrigerator – the okra will make it thicken on standing. Gently reheat, adding more water if it is too thick. Add the prawns and oysters just before serving.

PAELLA

🍴 SERVES 8–10 🥣 WORK TIME 1 HOUR ☕ COOKING TIME 40–45 MINUTES

EQUIPMENT

30–35 cm (12–14 inch) paella pan†   saucepan

2-pronged fork

chef's knife

small knife   bowls

small stiff brush

tea towel

wooden spoon

slotted spoon

chopping board

†large sauté or frying pan can also be used

ANNE SAYS
"*The traditional* paellera *is a wide, shallow, two-handled pan with sloping sides.*"

This Spanish dish is named after the paellera *in which it is cooked. Based on saffron-flavoured rice with chicken, shellfish, and spicy chorizo sausage, the variations are endless. It's a dish to feed a crowd, so invite your family or friends.*

GETTING AHEAD

The ingredients for paella can be prepared up to 2 hours ahead and kept, covered, in the refrigerator. Assemble and cook the paella just before serving.

metric	SHOPPING LIST	imperial
2	large onions	2
3	garlic cloves	3
2	red peppers	2
45–60 ml	boiling water	3–4 tbsp
2	large pinches of saffron threads	2
750 g	tomatoes	1 1/2 lb
500 g	raw, unpeeled jumbo prawns	1 lb
250 g	chorizo sausages	8 oz
375 g	French beans	12 oz
1 kg	mussels	2 lb
8–10	chicken legs, total weight about 750 g (1 1/2 lb)	8–10
	salt and pepper	
60 ml	olive oil	4 tbsp
750 g	short-grain rice, such as Arborio	1 1/2 lb
1.5 litres	water, more if needed	2 1/3 pints
15–30 ml	chopped parsley for decoration (optional)	1–2 tbsp

INGREDIENTS

chicken legs†
mussels

tomatoes
raw, unpeeled jumbo prawns

chorizo sausages   short-grain rice   red peppers

onions   garlic cloves

French beans   saffron threads   olive oil

†chicken thighs can also be used

ANNE SAYS
"*You can substitute Italian pepperoni or Arab merguez for the chorizo sausages.*"

ORDER OF WORK

1 **PREPARE THE INGREDIENTS**

2 **COOK THE PAELLA**

1 PREPARE THE INGREDIENTS

Saffron releases colour and flavour into hot water

1 Peel the onions, leaving a little of the root attached, and cut them lengthwise in half. Slice each half horizontally, then vertically, towards the root, leaving the slices attached at the root end. Finally, cut across to make small dice. Peel and finely chop the garlic; slice the peppers into thin strips (see box, right).

2 Put the boiling water in a small bowl and sprinkle in the saffron threads. Soak, at least 15 minutes.

3 Meanwhile, cut the cores from the tomatoes and score an "x" on the base of each. Immerse in boiling water until the skins start to split, 8–15 seconds, depending on their ripeness. Transfer at once to cold water. When cool, peel off the skins. Cut them crosswise in half, squeeze out the seeds, then coarsely chop each half.

4 Leaving the prawns in their shells, pull off and discard their legs. Twist the central flange of each prawn tail and pull gently to remove the dark intestinal vein. Rinse and dry them.

Prawns are cooked in their shells for extra flavour

Gently twist and pull central tail flange to remove intestinal vein from prawns

HOW TO CORE AND SEED PEPPERS, AND CUT THEM INTO STRIPS OR DICE

The cores and seeds of peppers should be discarded before cutting peppers into strips or dice.

1 With a small knife, cut around the core of the bell pepper. Twist the core, and pull it out.

2 Halve the pepper lengthwise, and scrape out the seeds. Cut away the white ribs on the inside.

3 Set each pepper half cut-side down, flatten it with the heel of your hand, and, using a chef's knife, slice it lengthwise into thin strips. For dice, gather the strips together, and cut crosswise.

5 With the chef's knife, trim each of the chorizo sausages and cut them crosswise, on the diagonal, into 1 cm (3/8 inch) slices.

Smoked chorizo sausages have dark skins

6 With your fingers, snap off the stalk ends from the beans, pulling away any strings from both sides. Gather several beans together in a pile and cut them crosswise, on the diagonal, into 2.5 cm (1 inch) pieces.

7 Scrub each of the mussels under cold running water with the small stiff brush. Scrape the shells with the small knife to remove any barnacles. Detach and discard any weeds or "beards" from the mussel shells.

! TAKE CARE !
Discard any mussels that have broken shells or that do not close when tapped.

2 COOK THE PAELLA

1 Season the chicken with salt and pepper. Heat the oil in the paella pan and sauté the chicken, turning once, until brown and partially cooked, 10–12 minutes. Transfer to a plate.

2 Add the sliced chorizo sausage to the oil in the pan and sauté until browned, 1–2 minutes on each side. Transfer to the plate, using the slotted spoon, and reserve.

Red pepper strips become soft while they are sautéing

ANNE SAYS
"Frying the rice in oil helps to keep the grains separate during cooking."

3 Add the diced onion and the red pepper strips to the pan; cook, stirring occasionally with the wooden spoon, until soft, 5–7 minutes. Stir in the rice and cook until the grains absorb the oil, 2–3 minutes.

5 Arrange the prawns and mussels on the beans. Bring to a boil. Simmer, uncovered, until all the liquid has evaporated and the rice is tender but slightly chewy, 25–30 minutes. Turn the pan 90° every 7 minutes so the paella cooks evenly.

 TO SERVE
Sprinkle the paella with parsley, if you like, and serve on warmed plates.

4 Stir in the water, garlic, saffron with its soaking liquid, plenty of salt, and pepper. Push the chicken pieces down into the rice mixture. Scatter the chorizo sausage slices over the rice, followed by the chopped tomatoes, and then the beans.

! TAKE CARE !
Do not stir the paella during cooking or the rice will become sticky.

6 If the rice is undercooked when the liquid has evaporated, add a little more water and continue simmering, a few minutes longer. Remove from the heat, and discard any mussels that have not opened. Cover with the tea towel, and let stand, 5 minutes.

Rice should be just tender with separate grains

VARIATION

SEAFOOD PAELLA
In this version of paella, the chicken is replaced by squid.

1 Omit the French beans and the chicken legs. Prepare the saffron, onions, garlic, tomatoes, and chorizo sausages as directed, substituting green peppers for the red, and using clams in place of the mussels.
2 With the prawns in their shells, hold each one, underside up on a chopping board. Leaving the tail end intact, cut the prawns in half to open in a butterfly shape. Remove the dark intestinal vein.
3 Rinse 375 g (12 oz) cleaned squid and drain it. Cut the tentacles from the body and cut them into 2–3 pieces if large, or leave whole if small. Cut the body across into 1 cm ($^3/_8$ inch) rings.
4 Cook the chorizo sausages, onions, green peppers, and rice as directed. Pour in the water, arrange the chorizo slices over the rice, followed by the prawns, tomatoes, squid, 125 g (4 oz) shelled fresh or defrosted peas, and finally the clams. Cook and serve as directed.

ANNE SAYS
"Tradition has it that the diners wait for the paella, never does the paella wait for the diners!"

FIVE-SPICE FILLET OF SALMON

🍽 SERVES 4 🥣 WORK TIME 30–35 MINUTES 🍲 BAKING TIME 20–25 MINUTES

EQUIPMENT

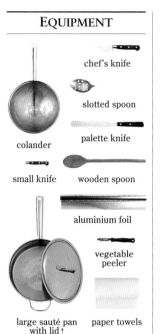

chef's knife

slotted spoon

palette knife

colander

small knife   wooden spoon

aluminium foil

vegetable peeler

large sauté pan   paper towels
with lid †

small
bowl
large baking dish

greaseproof paper

chopping board

†large frying pan with lid can also
be used

Pieces of salmon are coated with spices, lightly pan-fried, then baked on a bed of julienne vegetables. I like to use Chinese five-spice powder, but the same method will also suit curry powder or your favourite blend of Indian spices.

GETTING AHEAD
The vegetables can be prepared up to 1 day ahead, and kept, covered, in the refrigerator. Do not assemble the casserole or cook the fish until just before serving.

INGREDIENTS

salmon
fillets   dry white wine

ground
fennel seed   leeks

Chinese
five-spice   carrots   cayenne
powder   pepper

butter   courgettes

metric	SHOPPING LIST	imperial
375 g	carrots	12 oz
750 g	courgettes	1½ lb
750 g	leeks	1½ lb
60 g	butter, more if needed	2 oz
	salt and pepper	
4	pieces of skinless salmon fillet (weighing about 175 g/6 oz each)	4
30 ml	dry white wine	2 tbsp
	For the spice mixture	
15 ml	Chinese five-spice powder	1 tbsp
15 ml	ground fennel seed	1 tbsp
1	pinch of cayenne pepper	1

ORDER OF WORK

1 PREPARE AND COOK THE VEGETABLE JULIENNE

2 PREPARE THE SALMON AND BAKE THE CASSEROLE

1 PREPARE AND COOK THE VEGETABLE JULIENNE

Carrots are easy to slice thinly once sides are squared off

1 Peel and trim each of the carrots. With the chef's knife, cut them into 7.5 cm (3 inch) lengths and square off the sides. Cut each piece lengthwise into fine slices.

2 Stack the slices and cut them lengthwise into fine julienne, keeping the tip of the knife on the board as you slice.

3 Trim the courgettes and cut each of them into 7.5 cm (3 inch) lengths. Cut off the peel , including about 3 mm (1/8 inch) of flesh.

4 Cut the slices of peel lengthwise into fine strips. Discard the interior pieces from the courgettes.

ANNE SAYS
"Cut vegetables into uniform, very fine strips so they will cook quickly and evenly."

5 Trim the leeks, discarding the roots and tough green tops. Cut them into 7.5 cm (3 inch) lengths, then cut lengthwise in half. Fan each half slightly, and cut lengthwise into thin julienne strips. Wash the strips in the colander very thoroughly.

Julienne should be cut into the finest possible slices

6 Melt half of the butter in the sauté pan. Add the leeks, carrots, salt, and pepper. Press a piece of buttered foil on top, cover with the lid, and cook gently, stirring occasionally, about 10 minutes.

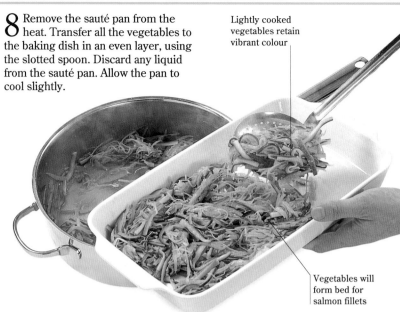

8 Remove the sauté pan from the heat. Transfer all the vegetables to the baking dish in an even layer, using the slotted spoon. Discard any liquid from the sauté pan. Allow the pan to cool slightly.

Lightly cooked vegetables retain vibrant colour

Vegetables will form bed for salmon fillets

7 Add the courgette julienne, cover with the foil again, and continue cooking until all the vegetables are tender, stirring occasionally, 8–10 minutes longer.

! TAKE CARE !
The vegetables should steam gently in their own juices without browning.

2 PREPARE THE SALMON AND BAKE THE CASSEROLE

1 Heat the oven to 200°C (400°F, Gas 6). Rinse the salmon under cold water and dry with paper towels.

2 Combine the Chinese five-spice powder, ground fennel seed, cayenne pepper, and a pinch of salt. Sprinkle the spices onto a sheet of greaseproof paper.

3 Coat the sides of each piece of salmon with the spice mixture, patting the fish gently with your hands so it is evenly coated.

4 Heat the remaining butter in the sauté pan. Cook the salmon over high heat, turning once with the palette knife, 1–2 minutes on each side.

5 Transfer the salmon to the baking dish, using the palette knife to place the pieces on the vegetables.

Sprinkling of white wine adds flavour

6 Sprinkle each piece of salmon with a little of the white wine. Bake the salmon and vegetables in the heated oven, 20–25 minutes.

7 When done, the salmon flesh should just flake when tested with a fork.

†◎¶ TO SERVE
Pile the vegetable julienne on warmed individual plates and set one piece of salmon on top of each. Decorate with lemon slices, if you like.

Vegetable julienne complements the flavour of spice-coated salmon

V A R I A T I O N

SALMON FILLETS WITH MUSHROOM AND LEEK JULIENNE

The spice coating is omitted to show off the pretty pink of the salmon, while a julienne of mushrooms replaces the carrots and courgettes.

1 Omit the courgettes, carrots, and spice mixture. Cut the leeks as directed. Wipe 375 g (12 oz) mushrooms with damp paper towels and trim the stalks even with the caps. Set the mushrooms stalk-side down on a chopping board and thinly slice them. Stack the slices and cut into very thin strips.

2 Cook the leeks as directed, add the mushrooms, and continue cooking, uncovered, until all the liquid from the vegetables has evaporated, 5–8 minutes longer.

3 Transfer the vegetables to individual baking dishes. Rinse the salmon as directed, season with salt and pepper, and set one piece of fish in each dish of vegetables.

4 Sprinkle each piece of fish with a little of the white wine and bake as directed.

Five-spice powder adds depth of flavour to salmon fillet

SEAFOOD AND TOMATO STEW

Cioppino

 SERVES 4   WORK TIME 45–50 MINUTES   COOKING TIME 20–25 MINUTES

EQUIPMENT

bowls

 colander

kitchen string   crab crackers†

chef's knife

small stiff brush

small knife

saucepans, 1 with lid

large flameproof casserole, with lid

wooden spoon

slotted spoon

chopping board

†nutcrackers can also be used

Cioppino is a hearty seafood stew, created by Italian immigrants in San Francisco in the nineteenth century. The fragrant tomato broth is full of crabs, mussels, scallops, and white fish.

GETTING AHEAD

The broth can be made and the shellfish and fish can be prepared up to 4 hours ahead, and kept, covered, in the refrigerator. Assemble and cook the stew just before serving because the seafood toughens if overcooked.

metric	SHOPPING LIST	imperial
1.4 kg	tomatoes	3 lb
3	garlic cloves	3
2	large onions	2
60 ml	olive oil	4 tbsp
15 ml	tomato purée	1 tbsp
1	pinch of cayenne pepper	1
	salt and pepper	
1	bouquet garni, made with 5–6 parsley stalks, 2–3 sprigs of fresh thyme, and 1 bay leaf	1
500 ml	dry white wine	16 fl oz
2	whole cooked medium crabs, total weight about 1.4 kg (3 lb)	2
750 g	mussels	1½ lb
500 g	skinned white fish fillets	1 lb
250 g	scallops	8 oz
1	small bunch of parsley	1

INGREDIENTS

crabs   white fish fillets†

parsley   bouquet garni

    tomato purée

mussels   scallops

   tomatoes‡

olive oil   cayenne   dry white wine

onions   garlic cloves

† halibut, hake, or cod can be used

‡ a 850 g (28 oz) can whole plum tomatoes can also be used

ORDER OF WORK

1 MAKE THE TOMATO BROTH

2 PREPARE THE SHELLFISH AND FISH

3 COOK THE CIOPPINO

1 MAKE THE TOMATO BROTH

1 Peel, seed, and chop the tomatoes (see box, right). Set the flat side of the chef's knife on top of each garlic clove and strike it with your fist. Discard the skin and finely chop the garlic.

Garlic skin peels off easily if cloves have been lightly crushed beforehand

2 Peel the onions, leaving a little of the root attached, and cut them lengthwise in half. Lay each onion half flat on the chopping board and slice horizontally, then vertically, towards the root, leaving the slices attached at the root end. Cut across into dice.

3 Heat the oil in a medium saucepan, add the onions, and cook until soft and translucent, 3–5 minutes.

4 Add the tomato purée, chopped tomatoes, garlic, cayenne, salt, pepper, and bouquet garni to the pan; pour in the white wine. Cover and simmer, stirring occasionally, about 20 minutes. Meanwhile, prepare the shellfish and fish.

White wine moistens tomatoes, onions, and garlic for broth

Bouquet garni of fresh herbs adds aromatic flavour

HOW TO PEEL, SEED, AND CHOP TOMATOES

Tomatoes are frequently peeled and seeded before chopping so they need not be strained after cooking.

1 Bring a pan of water to a boil. Using a small knife, cut out the cores from the tomatoes. Score an "x" on the base of each. Immerse in the water until the skins start to split, 8–15 seconds depending on their ripeness. Using a slotted spoon, transfer them at once to cold water to stop cooking.

2 When cool, peel the skin from the tomatoes with a small knife. Cut them crosswise in half and squeeze out the seeds.

3 Set each tomato half cut-side down and slice it. Give it a half turn and slice again. Chop the flesh coarsely or finely, as required.

2 PREPARE THE SHELLFISH AND FISH

1 Set one of the crabs, back down, on the chopping board. Twist off each of the legs with your fingers and reserve.

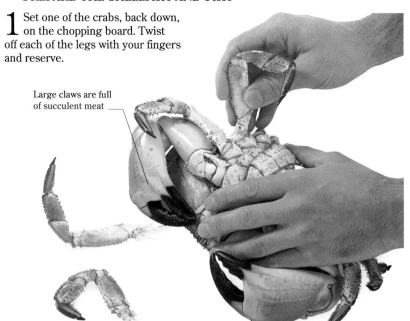

Large claws are full of succulent meat

2 Holding the crab body steady, twist off the claws at the bottom joint and reserve with the crab legs.

3 Using the crab crackers, crack the claws, leaving them whole and taking care not to crush the meat. If the legs are large, crack them also; discard them if they are small.

4 Open the body: with your fingers, lift off and discard the "apron" flap from the centre of the shell.

Body section separates easily from hard shell

5 With your thumbs, push along the "perforation" to crack the central section of the shell under the tail and prise it apart.

Soft gills are known as "dead men's fingers"

6 Gently pull the central body section away from the hard shell with one hand. Scrape out any soft brown meat from inside the shell, using a teaspoon, and reserve in a bowl; discard the shell.

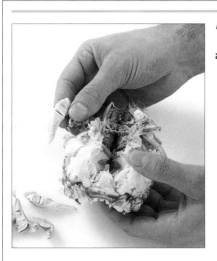

7 With your fingers, pull off the soft gills from the central body section and discard them.

8 Crack the central body section in half, using the chef's knife: while pushing the knife handle down with one hand, steady the end of the blade on the board with your other hand.

Apply pressure to knife with both hands to crack central body of crab

9 Pick out the meat from the central body section with the end of a teaspoon, discarding small pieces of cartilage. Add to the crab meat in the bowl and reserve. Repeat the whole process with the second crab.

Handle end of teaspoon is handy "pick" for removing crab meat

Crab meat flakes easily into bowl

10 Scrub the mussels thoroughly under cold running water with the small stiff brush.

11 Discard any mussels that have broken shells or that do not close when tapped.

Stringy "beards" must be removed from mussels

12 With the small knife, scrape the mussels to remove any barnacles. Detach and discard any weeds or "beards" from the shells.

13 Rinse the fish fillets under cold running water and dry them. Set the fillets on the chopping board and cut them into 5 cm (2 inch) pieces.

Fish is cut into large chunks that hold their shape during cooking

Use sawing action to cut through fish without tearing flesh

14 If necessary, discard the tough crescent-shaped membrane at the side of each scallop. Rinse the scallops in a bowl of cold water. Transfer to the colander and let them drain thoroughly.

3 COOK THE CIOPPINO

1 Discard the bouquet garni from the broth. Taste and adjust the seasoning; it should be quite peppery.

3 Ladle the hot tomato broth over the seafood and add water, if necessary, so the seafood is just covered. Cover the casserole with the lid and bring to a boil. Simmer until the mussels have opened and the white fish flakes easily with a fork, 3–5 minutes.

Tomato broth permeates layers of seafood during cooking

2 Pack the fish pieces into the bottom of the casserole in an even layer, followed by the scallops. Arrange the crab meat and the cracked crab legs and claws over the scallops. Finally, cover with the mussels.

ANNE SAYS
"*Do not overcook the stew or the shellfish will be tough and the white fish will fall apart.*"

4 Meanwhile, strip the parsley leaves from the stalks and pile the leaves on the chopping board. With the chef's knife, finely chop the leaves.

Peppery broth is rich with flavour of fish and shellfish

Opened mussel shells release their flavour into stew

5 Discard any mussels that have not opened. Taste the cioppino for seasoning and adjust if necessary.

🍽 **TO SERVE**
Transfer the cioppino to warmed bowls with one crab claw in each bowl. Sprinkle with the chopped parsley. Serve immediately, with slices of sourdough bread, if you like.

Tomato broth joins with a variety of seafood in this full-flavoured stew

Sourdough bread is traditional with cioppino for soaking up the tasty broth

VARIATION
FISH CIOPPINO
Traditional cioppino always includes shellfish, but I like to make this delicious stew using a variety of firm fish.

1 Make the tomato broth as directed. Omit the parsley. Chop the leaves from 1 small bunch of fresh basil.
2 Omit the crabs, mussels, and scallops. Prepare 500 g (1 lb) halibut or cod fillets as directed. Discard the skin from 500 g (1 lb) tuna steak, rinse with cold water, and dry with paper towels. Cut the tuna into 2.5 cm (1 inch) cubes.
3 Prepare 500 g (1 lb) monkfish fillets: if necessary, remove the membrane that covers the flesh of the fillets. Rinse the monkfish under cold water and dry with paper towels. Holding the fillets steady, cut into diagonal slices, about 1.25 cm (½ inch) thick.
4 Layer the fish in a saucepan, starting with the monkfish, followed by the tuna, then the halibut or cod.
5 Add half of the basil to the tomato broth, then ladle the broth over the fish and simmer until all the fish flakes easily with a fork, 10–12 minutes. Serve in warmed individual shallow bowls and sprinkle with the remaining basil. Breadsticks make a good accompaniment. Serves 6.

CHICKEN PAPRIKA WITH CARAWAY DUMPLINGS

¶◉¶ SERVES 4–6 ⌣ WORK TIME 40–45 MINUTES ⌣ COOKING TIME 35–40 MINUTES

EQUIPMENT

bowls

wide shallow saucepan, with lid

paper towels

large flameproof casserole, with lid

sieve

wooden spoon

slotted spoon

chef's knife

saucepan

small knife

whisk

2-pronged fork

chopping board

Good-quality Hungarian paprika is the key to this rich stew with caraway-seed dumplings. Steamed mangetout are a contemporary accompaniment.

GETTING AHEAD

The stew can be prepared up to 1 day ahead and kept, covered, in the refrigerator; add the soured cream and make the dumplings just before serving.

metric	SHOPPING LIST	imperial
1	large onion	1
2	garlic cloves	2
500 g	tomatoes	1 lb
1.6 kg	chicken, jointed into 8 pieces	3½ lb
	salt and pepper	
30 ml	vegetable oil	2 tbsp
30 ml	paprika, more to taste	2 tbsp
15 ml	plain flour	1 tbsp
500 ml	chicken stock (see box, page 57), more if needed	16 fl oz
125 ml	soured cream	4 fl oz
	For the caraway dumplings	
100 g	plain flour	3¼ oz
1.25 ml	baking powder	¼ tsp
2.5 ml	salt	½ tsp
10 ml	caraway seeds	2 tsp
2	eggs	2
150 ml	water, more if needed	5 fl oz

INGREDIENTS

chicken pieces

vegetable oil

plain flour

chicken stock †

paprika

caraway seeds

garlic cloves

onion

soured cream

baking powder

tomatoes

eggs

† water can also be used

ORDER OF WORK

1 PREPARE THE DUMPLINGS AND VEGETABLES

2 COOK THE CHICKEN AND DUMPLINGS

1 PREPARE THE DUMPLINGS AND VEGETABLES

1 Sift the flour, baking powder, and salt together into a large bowl.

2 Mix in the caraway seeds. Make a well in the centre of the flour mixture, using your fingers.

Caraway seeds add characteristic Hungarian flavour to dumplings

Eggs in batter make dumplings light

Flour will blend easily with eggs if drawn in gradually

3 In a small bowl, whisk the eggs together. Add to the well with about three-quarters of the water. Gradually draw in the flour and stir just until combined. Add more water if the dough is dry. Cover and refrigerate while preparing the vegetables.

ANNE SAYS
"Add enough liquid so that the dough is moist, but not too soft."

4 Peel the onion and cut it lengthwise in half. Set each half cut-side down and slice horizontally, then vertically, towards the root. Cut across to make fine dice.

Curled fingers guide knife blade

Coarsely chopped tomatoes will cook down in stew

5 Set the flat side of the chef's knife on top of each garlic clove and strike it with your fist. Discard the skin and finely chop the garlic.

6 Cut out the cores and score an "x" on the tomatoes. Immerse in boiling water until the skins split, 8–15 seconds. Transfer to cold water. Peel and halve them; squeeze out the seeds and coarsely chop.

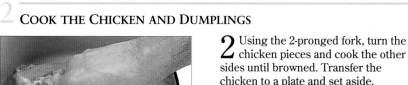

2 COOK THE CHICKEN AND DUMPLINGS

2 Using the 2-pronged fork, turn the chicken pieces and cook the other sides until browned. Transfer the chicken to a plate and set aside.

1 Heat the oven to 180°C (350°F, Gas 4). Season the chicken pieces with salt and pepper. Heat the oil in the casserole on top of the stove. Working in batches, if necessary, add the chicken to the casserole, skin-side down, and brown well, about 5 minutes.

Browning chicken intensifies flavour of sauce

3 Add the chopped onion to the casserole and cook over medium heat, stirring occasionally, until soft, 2–3 minutes. Add the garlic and continue cooking, 3–5 minutes longer.

4 Stir in the paprika. Cook very gently, stirring occasionally, about 5 minutes. Stir in the flour. Then add the tomatoes, chicken stock, salt, and pepper; bring the mixture to a boil.

5 Return the browned chicken pieces to the casserole. Cover with the lid and cook in the heated oven until the chicken is tender when pierced with the 2-pronged fork, 35–40 minutes.

6 Meanwhile, cook the caraway dumplings: bring the shallow saucepan, filled with salted water, to a boil. Take 2 small spoons, dip them first in the boiling water, then use them to shape the dumpling dough into 2 cm (³/₄ inch) balls; drop the balls into the boiling water.

ANNE SAYS
"If necessary, cook the dumplings in batches so the saucepan is not crowded."

Water should simmer but not boil vigorously

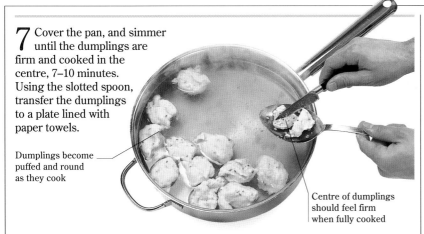

7 Cover the pan, and simmer until the dumplings are firm and cooked in the centre, 7–10 minutes. Using the slotted spoon, transfer the dumplings to a plate lined with paper towels.

Dumplings become puffed and round as they cook

Centre of dumplings should feel firm when fully cooked

8 Transfer the chicken pieces to a platter and keep warm. Stir the soured cream into the sauce and taste for seasoning. Add the dumplings to the casserole and turn each one so it is coated in sauce. Cover the casserole and cook very gently, about 2 minutes.

! TAKE CARE !
Do not heat the soured cream too vigorously or it may curdle.

🍽 **TO SERVE**
Divide the chicken among warmed plates; cover with the paprika sauce and dumplings.

Dumplings soak up the flavour and colour of paprika sauce

Crunchy green mangetout complement creamy stew

V A R I A T I O N
CHICKEN AND PAPRIKA PILAF

Long-grain rice and chicken marry in this rice pilaf perfumed with paprika and fresh oregano.

1 Omit the flour and soured cream; substitute 4 boneless chicken breasts (total weight about 750 g/1½ lb) for the whole chicken. Omit the dumplings.
2 Strip the leaves from 7–10 sprigs of fresh oregano, reserving 4 top sprigs for decoration. Finely chop the leaves. Prepare the onion, garlic, and tomatoes as directed. Core, seed, and dice 1 green pepper.
3 Season the chicken with salt and pepper. Heat the oil in a casserole on top of the stove. Brown the chicken well on both sides. Transfer to a plate.
4 Lower the heat, add the onion, garlic, and pepper; cook as directed.
5 Stir in the paprika and cook very gently, stirring occasionally, about 5 minutes. Add 300 g (10 oz) long-grain rice and cook, stirring, until the rice is slightly translucent, 2–3 minutes.
6 Add the chopped oregano, tomatoes, 30 ml (2 tbsp) tomato purée, 1 litre (1⅔ pints) chicken stock or water, and the chicken breasts. Cover, and cook in the heated oven until the chicken is tender and the rice is cooked, 20–25 minutes.
7 Taste for seasoning. Cut each chicken breast into 7–8 diagonal slices. Pile the rice on warmed plates, arrange the chicken on top, and decorate with the oregano sprigs. Serves 4.

CHICKEN AND BEER STEW

🍽 SERVES 4–6 🥣 WORK TIME 25–30 MINUTES 🍲 COOKING TIME 50–55 MINUTES

EQUIPMENT

large flameproof
casserole, with lid

rolling pin

plastic bag

wooden spoon

large metal spoon

2-pronged fork

chopping
board

chef's knife

small knife

paper towels

kitchen string

ANNE SAYS

"*You can use poultry shears instead of a chef's knife for jointing the chicken, if you prefer. They are especially good for splitting the breastbone, cutting the backbone and rib bones, and for cutting the breast and the legs in half.*"

The inspiration for this stew comes from northern Europe. The darker the beer, the richer this dish will be. Mashed potatoes would be a good accompaniment to the stew, and there's no mystery what you should serve to drink with it!

GETTING AHEAD

The stew can be prepared up to 2 days ahead and kept, covered, in the refrigerator; the flavour will mellow. Reheat it on top of the stove before serving.

INGREDIENTS

mushrooms

chicken†

plain flour

bouquet garni

parsley

butter

vegetable
oil

Cognac

beer

juniper
berries

onions

double
cream

†chicken already jointed into
8 pieces can also be used

metric	SHOPPING LIST	imperial
1	chicken, weighing about 1.6 kg (3½ lb)	1
750 g	onions	1½ lb
500 g	mushrooms	1 lb
10 ml	juniper berries	2 tsp
	salt and pepper	
30 g	butter	1 oz
30 ml	vegetable oil	2 tbsp
30 g	plain flour	1 oz
45–60 ml	Cognac	3–4 tbsp
1	bouquet garni, made with 5–6 parsley stalks, 2–3 sprigs of fresh thyme, and 1 bay leaf	1
750 ml	beer	1¼ pints
1	small bunch of parsley for garnish	1
60 ml	double cream	4 tbsp

ORDER OF WORK

1 PREPARE THE STEW
INGREDIENTS

2 COOK THE STEW

1 PREPARE THE STEW INGREDIENTS

Plastic bag stops juniper berries scattering on board

1 Joint the chicken into 8 pieces (see box, below). Peel the onions, leaving a little of the root attached, then cut them lengthwise in half. Lay each half flat on the chopping board and cut across into thin slices.

2 Wipe the mushroom caps with damp paper towels and trim the stalks even with the caps. Set the mushrooms stalk-side down on the chopping board and, with the small knife, cut them into quarters.

3 Put the juniper berries inside the plastic bag. Holding the end of the bag closed in one hand, crush the berries gently with the rolling pin in order to release their flavour.

HOW TO JOINT A CHICKEN INTO 8 PIECES

1 Using a chef's knife, cut down between one leg joint and the body. Twist the leg sharply outwards to break the joint, then cut through it and pull the leg from the body. Repeat this procedure for the other leg.

2 Slit closely along both sides of the breastbone to loosen the meat, then split the breastbone. Turn the bird over onto its breast and cut along one side of the backbone. The bird is now divided in half.

3 Cut the backbone and rib bones in one piece from the breast half where they are still attached, leaving the wing joints attached to the breast.

4 Cut each breast piece in half diagonally, cutting through the breast and rib bones so that a portion of the breast meat is included with the wing. Cut off any sharp bones.

5 Cut each leg in half through the joint, between the thigh and the drumstick, using the line of white fat around the joint as a guide.

2 COOK THE STEW

Remove chicken
pieces as they brown

Heavy-based
casserole gives
even heat

1 Season the chicken pieces with salt and pepper. Heat the butter and oil in the casserole until foaming, and add the chicken pieces, skin-side down. Brown them well, about 5 minutes.

2 Turn the chicken pieces over, using the 2-pronged fork, and brown the other side. Transfer the chicken to a plate and reserve.

3 Add the sliced onions and cook, stirring occasionally, until soft and well browned, 10–15 minutes. Sprinkle with the flour and cook, stirring, until the flour is just lightly browned, 1–2 minutes. Return the browned chicken to the pan in a single layer.

4 Add the Cognac. Set the alcohol alight with a lighted match. Baste the chicken with the Cognac until the flames subside, 20–30 seconds.

! TAKE CARE !
Flames can rise quite high, so stand back and use a long-handled spoon for basting.

5 Add the mushroom quarters, bouquet garni, and crushed juniper berries to the casserole. Pour in the beer.

Alcohol in beer evaporates
during cooking, leaving
rich concentrated taste

6 Bring to a boil, cover, and simmer until the chicken is tender when pierced with the 2-pronged fork and the juices run clear, 40–50 minutes.

7 Meanwhile, strip the parsley leaves from the stalks and pile the leaves on the chopping board. With the chef's knife, finely chop them.

Cream stirred into stew gives sauce velvety consistency

8 Discard the bouquet garni from the stew and skim off excess fat from the surface using the large metal spoon.

9 Stir in the cream, and bring back just to a boil. Taste the stew for seasoning and adjust if needed.

¡O¡ TO SERVE
Transfer the stew to a warmed serving bowl, garnish it with the parsley, and serve immediately.

Mushrooms and onions add extra flavour

Dark beer creates a rich flavourful sauce

VARIATION
CHICKEN WITH COGNAC

In this stew, the amount of Cognac is increased and chicken stock replaces the beer, with whole pickling onions instead of sliced onions.

1 Omit the mushrooms, onions, beer, juniper berries, cream, and parsley. Joint the chicken as directed. Put 500 g (1 lb) pickling onions in a bowl, cover with boiling water; let stand, 2 minutes. Remove the onions and peel them, leaving a little of the root attached to hold the onion together while cooking.

2 Brown the chicken as directed; set aside. Add the onions to the casserole and cook, stirring, until golden brown, 5–7 minutes. Transfer to a bowl.

3 Sprinkle the flour into the casserole and cook, 1–2 minutes. Replace the chicken and increase the heat to medium-high. Add 250 ml (8 fl oz) Cognac and bring to a boil. Hold a lighted match to the side of the casserole to set the alcohol alight. Baste the chicken with the sauce until the flames subside, 20–30 seconds.

4 Add 250 ml (8 fl oz) chicken stock, the onions, bouquet garni, salt, and pepper and cook as directed.

5 Discard the bouquet garni and taste the stew for seasoning. Arrange the chicken on 4–6 warmed individual plates and spoon over the onions and sauce. Serve immediately, with new potatoes tossed in chopped parsley, if you like.

CHICKEN IN A POT

Poule au Pot

🍽 SERVES 4–6   🥄 WORK TIME 1 HOUR   ♨ COOKING TIME 1¼–1½ HOURS

EQUIPMENT

bowls

heatproof plate

aluminium foil

muslin

kitchen string

paper towels

large metal spoon

vegetable peeler

slotted spoon

small knife

chef's knife

2-pronged fork

chopping board

whisk

sieves

saucepan

trussing needle

large flameproof casserole, with lid

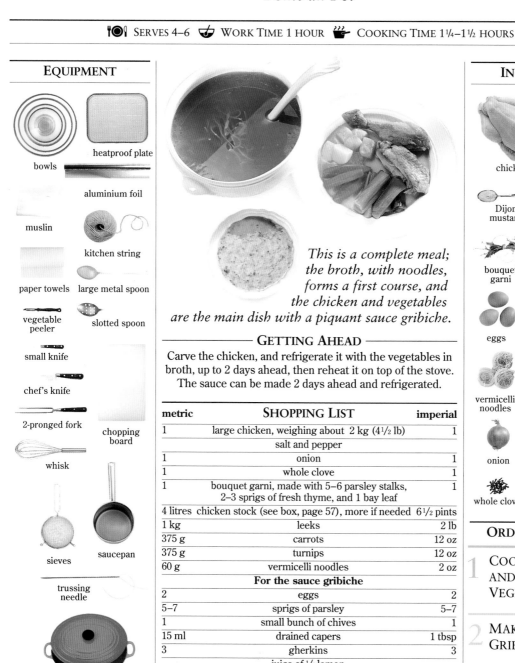

This is a complete meal; the broth, with noodles, forms a first course, and the chicken and vegetables are the main dish with a piquant sauce gribiche.

GETTING AHEAD

Carve the chicken, and refrigerate it with the vegetables in broth, up to 2 days ahead, then reheat it on top of the stove. The sauce can be made 2 days ahead and refrigerated.

metric	SHOPPING LIST	imperial
1	large chicken, weighing about 2 kg (4½ lb)	1
	salt and pepper	
1	onion	1
1	whole clove	1
1	bouquet garni, made with 5–6 parsley stalks, 2–3 sprigs of fresh thyme, and 1 bay leaf	1
4 litres	chicken stock (see box, page 57), more if needed	6½ pints
1 kg	leeks	2 lb
375 g	carrots	12 oz
375 g	turnips	12 oz
60 g	vermicelli noodles	2 oz
For the sauce gribiche		
2	eggs	2
5–7	sprigs of parsley	5–7
1	small bunch of chives	1
15 ml	drained capers	1 tbsp
3	gherkins	3
	juice of ½ lemon	
5 ml	Dijon mustard	1 tsp
30 ml	dry white wine	2 tbsp
250 ml	vegetable oil	8 fl oz

INGREDIENTS

chicken

parsley

chives

Dijon mustard

leeks

bouquet garni

gherkins

turnips

eggs

carrots

chicken stock

vermicelli noodles

vegetable oil

lemon juice

onion

capers

whole clove

white wine

ORDER OF WORK

1 COOK CHICKEN AND PREPARE VEGETABLES

2 MAKE THE SAUCE GRIBICHE

3 FINISH THE DISH

1 COOK CHICKEN AND PREPARE VEGETABLES

2 Put the chicken in the casserole. Add the bouquet garni and clove-studded onion; pour in enough chicken stock to cover the chicken by about three-quarters. Bring the stock to a boil, cover the casserole, and simmer, 45 minutes. Meanwhile, prepare the vegetables.

ANNE SAYS
"The stock should just cover the thighs so that they cook more quickly, and the tender breast does not overcook."

Stock surrounds chicken and ensures even cooking

1 Truss the chicken (see box, page 46). Trim the root and stalk end from the onion, and peel it, using the small knife. Stud it with the clove.

3 Trim the leeks, discarding the roots and tough green tops. Slit them lengthwise with the chef's knife and wash thoroughly under cold water. Cut them into 7.5 cm (3 inch) lengths and put on a large piece of muslin. Gather up the edges and tie securely with string to make a bundle that is easy to remove at the end of cooking.

Turnips should be firm and heavy in the hand

4 Trim the carrots and cut into 7.5 cm (3 inch) lengths. Halve them lengthwise and trim the edges so they are rounded. Tie them in a piece of muslin as for the leeks.

5 Peel the turnips and square off the sides; cut them into 2.5 cm (1 inch) slices. Stack the slices and cut into 2.5 cm (1 inch) strips. Cut the strips crosswise into 2.5 cm (1 inch) cubes. Tie them in muslin as for the leeks.

Vegetable bundles will be easy to remove at end of cooking

6 Add the vegetable bundles to the chicken with more stock so they are covered. Cover the casserole and simmer until the chicken and vegetables are cooked, 25–30 minutes longer. Meanwhile, make the sauce gribiche (see page 47).

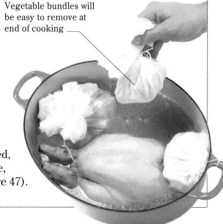

HOW TO TRUSS A CHICKEN

1 Wipe the inside of the chicken with paper towels and season it, inside and out, with salt and pepper.

Hold chicken steady with one hand

2 Fold back the neck skin and, using the point of a small knife, remove the wishbone by cutting it out. Thread a trussing needle with string.

Chicken breast will be easy to carve into slices if wishbone is removed before cooking

3 Set the bird, breast-side up; push the legs well back and down so the ends are straight up. Insert the trussing needle into the flesh at the knee joint, push it through the bird, and out through the other knee joint.

4 Turn the bird over. Pull the neck skin over the neck cavity, and tuck the wing tips over it. Push the needle through both sections of one wing, into the neck skin, and under the backbone to the other side. Repeat with the second wing.

5 Turn the bird onto its side. Pull the string firmly together and tie securely. Turn the bird breast-side up. Tuck the tail into the cavity of the bird and fold over the top skin. Push the needle through the skin.

Chicken legs will not overcook once bird is trussed

Catch ends of drumsticks in loops of string

6 Loop the string around one of the drumsticks, under the breastbone, and over the other drumstick. Tie the ends of string together securely.

ANNE SAYS
"Trussing keeps the chicken in shape so it cooks evenly."

2 MAKE THE SAUCE GRIBICHE

1 Boil the eggs, 10 minutes. Drain, cool, and shell them. Rinse with cold water.

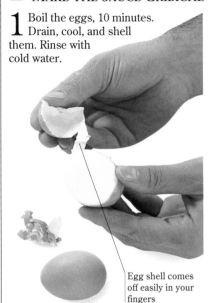

Egg shell comes off easily in your fingers

2 Dry the eggs and separate the yolks from the whites by gently pulling them apart. Cut the whites into strips and finely chop them.

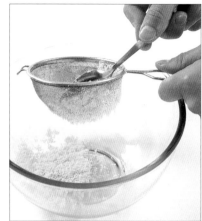

3 Put the yolks in a small sieve set over a bowl and work them through, using the back of a kitchen spoon. Scrape away the yolk clinging to the bottom of the sieve.

4 Strip the parsley leaves from the stalks. Pile the leaves on the chopping board and finely chop them with the chef's knife. Gather the chives into a pile, and finely chop them; mix them with the parsley.

Finely chopped capers will blend into sauce

5 With the chef's knife, finely chop the capers. Cut the gherkins crosswise into slices, then finely chop them, and mix with the capers.

6 Add the lemon juice to the egg yolks with the mustard, salt, pepper, and white wine; whisk until combined. Gradually pour in the oil, while constantly whisking.

ANNE SAYS
"The sauce should emulsify and thicken slightly as you whisk."

7 Add the chopped egg whites, capers, gherkins, and herbs; whisk together to combine. Taste for seasoning.

3 FINISH THE DISH

1 Transfer the chicken to the chopping board, and remove the trussing string. Carve the chicken, using the chef's knife and the 2-pronged fork: cut down between one leg and the body. Turn the bird on its side and cut around the "oyster" meat so it remains attached to the thigh. Twist the leg sharply outwards to break the joint, then cut through it, and pull the leg from the body.

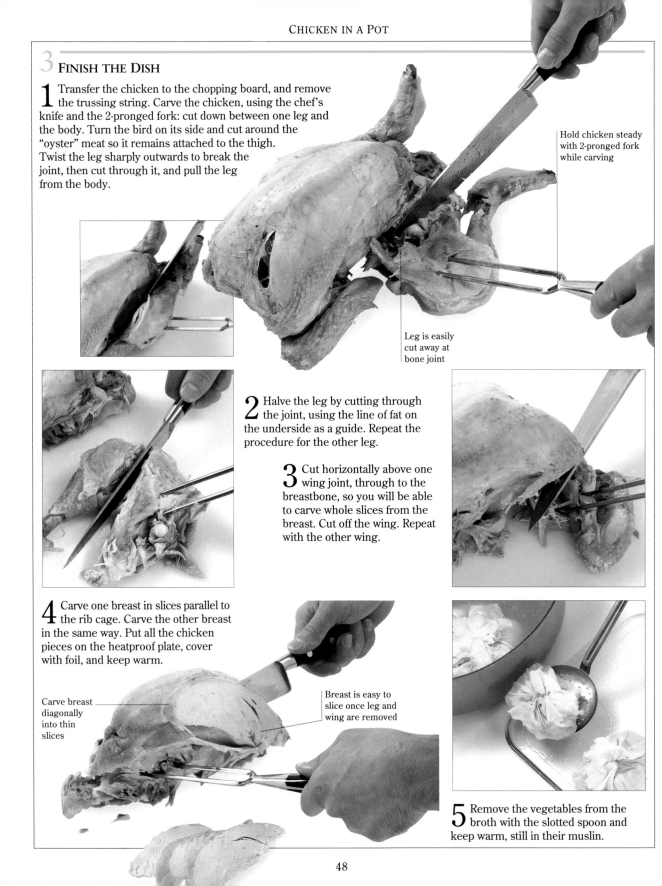

Hold chicken steady with 2-pronged fork while carving

Leg is easily cut away at bone joint

2 Halve the leg by cutting through the joint, using the line of fat on the underside as a guide. Repeat the procedure for the other leg.

3 Cut horizontally above one wing joint, through to the breastbone, so you will be able to carve whole slices from the breast. Cut off the wing. Repeat with the other wing.

4 Carve one breast in slices parallel to the rib cage. Carve the other breast in the same way. Put all the chicken pieces on the heatproof plate, cover with foil, and keep warm.

Carve breast diagonally into thin slices

Breast is easy to slice once leg and wing are removed

5 Remove the vegetables from the broth with the slotted spoon and keep warm, still in their muslin.

6 Strain the broth into the saucepan, bring to a boil, and simmer until well flavoured, 10–20 minutes. With the large metal spoon, skim off as much fat as possible and taste the broth for seasoning. Add the vermicelli noodles to the boiling broth and simmer just until tender, 3–5 minutes.

Broth is rich with flavour of chicken and vegetables

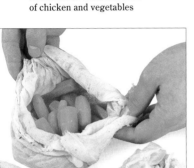

7 Meanwhile, cut the string from the bundles of carrots, leeks, and turnips, unwrap them, and discard the muslin. Cover the vegetables, and keep them warm, with the chicken, until ready to serve.

Rich-flavoured broth and noodles are served as a first course

¶◎¶ TO SERVE
Serve the broth and noodles as a first course, reserving 250 ml (8 fl oz) broth. Serve the chicken and vegetables as a main course, with the reserved broth. Serve the sauce gribiche separately.

Chicken and vegetables form the main course of this complete meal

Sauce gribiche, with gherkins and herbs, is a favourite accompaniment

V A R I A T I O N
TARRAGON CHICKEN

Here chicken is simmered with a generous amount of fresh tarragon, then the broth is transformed into a rich sauce.

1 Omit the leeks, carrots, and sauce gribiche. Truss the chicken as directed. Peel 750 g (1½ lb) turnips, cut into cubes, and tie them in 2 muslin bundles as directed.
2 Chop the leaves from 1 large bunch of fresh tarragon, reserving the stalks.
3 Cook the chicken as directed, with the tarragon stalks, stock, and the turnip bundles.
4 Carve the chicken as directed, cover, and keep warm. Lift out the turnips and keep warm.
5 Simmer the broth until reduced to about 500 ml (16 fl oz). Melt 60 g (2 oz) butter in a pan. Whisk in 30 g (1 oz) plain flour and cook until foaming, 30–60 seconds. Remove from the heat and cool slightly, then strain in the broth, and whisk to mix.
6 Return to the heat and cook, whisking constantly, until the sauce thickens; simmer, 1 minute longer.
7 Add 250 ml (8 fl oz) double cream. Simmer until slightly thickened, 2–3 minutes. Stir in the chopped tarragon and taste the sauce for seasoning.
8 Arrange the carved chicken and turnips on 4–6 warmed plates. Spoon some of the sauce over the chicken and serve the remainder separately.

TURKEY MOLE

🍽 SERVES 8 🥄 WORK TIME 45–50 MINUTES ♨ COOKING TIME 1¼–1¾ HOURS

EQUIPMENT

large flameproof
casserole, with lid

small frying
pan

saucepans

sieve

bowls

chef's knife

small knife

food processor †

2-pronged fork

vegetable
peeler

rubber spatula

chopping board

wooden spoon

ladle

†blender can also be used

*A blend of hot aromatic spices with bittersweet
chocolate gives character to this Mexican turkey
stew served with rice. Don't let the long
ingredient list deter you; this famous dish
is worth the attention.*

metric	SHOPPING LIST	imperial
1	celery stick	1
2	onions	2
1	carrot	1
4	garlic cloves	4
60 ml	vegetable oil	4 tbsp
1.6 kg	boneless turkey thighs	3½ lb
	salt and pepper	
1 litre	water	1⅔ pints
5 ml	black peppercorns	1 tsp
	For the mole purée	
500 g	tomatoes	1 lb
45 g	bittersweet chocolate	1½ oz
1	slice of stale white bread	1
1	stale corn tortilla	1
175 g	blanched almonds	6 oz
75 g	raisins	2½ oz
30 g	chilli powder	1 oz
5 ml	each ground cloves, coriander, and cumin	1 tsp
1.25 ml	ground aniseed	¼ tsp
10 ml	ground cinnamon	2 tsp
30 g	sesame seeds	1 oz

INGREDIENTS

carrot

tomatoes

vegetable
oil

raisins

onions

boneless
turkey thighs

blanched
almonds

sesame
seeds

chilli
powder

mixed
spices

cinnamon

aniseed

celery

garlic cloves

black
peppercorns

corn tortilla

white bread

bittersweet
chocolate

ORDER OF WORK

1 COOK THE TURKEY
AND FLAVOURINGS

2 PREPARE THE
MOLE PUREE

3 ASSEMBLE THE
TURKEY MOLE

1 COOK THE TURKEY AND FLAVOURINGS

1 Trim the celery stick, peel off the strings with the vegetable peeler, and cut the stick crosswise into quarters. Peel the onions and cut them into quarters. Peel the carrot and cut it crosswise into quarters.

Cut vegetables into large chunks so they do not break up during long cooking

2 Set the flat side of the chef's knife on top of each garlic clove and strike it with your fist. Peel off and discard the skin.

3 Season the turkey pieces with salt and pepper. Heat half of the oil in the casserole. Add the turkey pieces, skin-side down. Brown them well, turning occasionally, 10–15 minutes.

4 Add the water, celery, 4 onion quarters, 1 garlic clove, the peppercorns, and carrot. Bring to a boil, cover, and simmer until the turkey is very tender when pierced with the 2-pronged fork, 45–60 minutes. Meanwhile, prepare the mole purée.

Water should almost cover turkey and vegetables

Carrot adds slight sweetness to cooking liquid

2 PREPARE THE MOLE PUREE

1 Core the tomatoes and score an "x" on the base of each with the tip of the small knife. Immerse in boiling water until the skins start to split, 8–15 seconds, depending on their ripeness. Transfer to cold water. When cool, peel off the skins. Cut them crosswise in half, squeeze out the seeds, then coarsely chop each half.

2 Break the chocolate into pieces and coarsely chop them. Tear the bread and tortilla into pieces.

3 Combine the tomatoes in the food processor with the remaining onion quarters and garlic, the bread, tortilla, almonds, raisins, chilli powder, ground cloves, coriander, cumin, aniseed, cinnamon, and half of the sesame seeds. Work the ingredients to form a smooth purée.

ANNE SAYS
"If the mixture is very thick, or you are using a blender, add 125 ml (4 fl oz) water and purée the mixture in 2 batches."

Almonds add body to mixture for mole purée

! TAKE CARE !
Different chilli powders can vary greatly in strength, so be sure to check the type you are using before adding it to the mixture.

3 ASSEMBLE THE TURKEY MOLE

1 Remove the casserole from the heat, transfer the turkey thighs to a plate, and let cool slightly. Strain the cooking liquid into a bowl, discarding the vegetables.

2 When the turkey thighs are cool enough to handle, remove the skin and any fat, using the small knife. Pull the turkey meat into bite-sized pieces with your fingers.

Bittersweet chocolate adds depth of flavour to mole sauce

3 Heat the remaining oil in the casserole. Add the mole purée and cook, stirring constantly with the wooden spoon, until thick and dark, about 5 minutes.

4 Add the chocolate and cook, stirring constantly, to melt the chocolate into the purée, about 5 minutes longer.

5 Pour in the reserved cooking liquid, season with salt, and stir to combine. Simmer until the sauce begins to thicken, 25–30 minutes.

7 Return the turkey meat to the casserole and continue simmering until the sauce is thick enough to coat the back of the spoon, 10–15 minutes longer. Taste for seasoning.

Mole sauce should be dark and rich but not sticky

6 Meanwhile, toast the remaining sesame seeds: heat the frying pan, add the seeds, and toast them, stirring occasionally, until lightly browned, 2–3 minutes.

🍽 **TO SERVE**
Serve in warmed individual bowls, around white rice. Sprinkle with the toasted sesame seeds; top the rice with shredded coriander and chopped fresh chilli, if you like.

Warm flour tortillas are a good accompaniment to turkey mole

VARIATION

PORK MOLE

Mole sauce complements the mild flavour of pork, with a cooling accompaniment of soured cream.

1 Omit the turkey thighs, celery, carrots, and black peppercorns. Peel and quarter 1 onion. Peel 3 garlic cloves. Make the mole purée as directed. Cook the purée and chocolate, substituting 1 litre (1²/₃ pints) water for the turkey cooking liquid. Simmer until thickened, 25–30 minutes.
2 Meanwhile, trim the excess fat from 8 pork chops (weighing about 175 g/6 oz each) and season both sides with salt and pepper. Heat 30 ml (2 tbsp) oil in a large frying pan and brown the chops well over high heat, 1–2 minutes on each side. Add the chops to the mole sauce, cover, and cook gently until the pork is tender when pierced with a 2-pronged fork, 1–1¼ hours.
3 Toast the sesame seeds as directed. Taste the mole for seasoning. Divide the pork chops and sauce among 8 warmed plates, sprinkle with the toasted sesame seeds, and top each serving with 15 ml (1 tbsp) soured cream. Serve with white rice tossed with shredded coriander and chopped chilli, and kidney beans, and decorate with a coriander sprig, if you like.

— **GETTING AHEAD** —
The stew can be cooked 1–2 days ahead and kept, covered, in the refrigerator. Reheat it on top of the stove just before serving.

POUSSINS WITH PLUMS AND CABBAGE

EQUIPMENT

large flameproof casserole, with lid

colander

large pan

bowls

kitchen string

chef's knife

2-pronged fork

small knife

aluminium foil

wooden spoon

slotted spoon

whisk

chopping board

Small whole birds are cooked en cocotte *with Savoy cabbage. Bacon adds a smoky flavour to the sauce, with an underlying sweetness coming from fresh purple plums.*

GETTING AHEAD

The casserole can be cooked up to 1 day ahead and kept, covered, in the refrigerator. Reheat the birds with the cabbage in a 180°C (350°F, Gas 4) oven. Add the remaining plums and thicken the sauce just before serving.

INGREDIENTS

poussins

Savoy cabbage

bouquet garni

streaky bacon

arrowroot

purple plums

whole clove

dry white wine

chicken stock

vegetable oil

onion

ANNE SAYS
"*If 500 g (1 lb) birds are not available, use 3 larger ones, and serve half per person.*"

ORDER OF WORK

1 TIE UP THE BIRDS

2 BLANCH THE CABBAGE

3 ASSEMBLE AND BAKE THE DISH

4 FINISH THE DISH

metric	SHOPPING LIST	imperial
6	poussins, each weighing about 500 g (1 lb)	6
	salt and pepper	
1	Savoy cabbage, weighing about 1.4 kg (3 lb)	1
750 g	purple plums	1½ lb
250 g	streaky bacon rashers	8 oz
1	onion	1
1	whole clove	1
30 ml	vegetable oil	2 tbsp
1	bouquet garni (see box, page 58)	1
250 ml	dry white wine	8 fl oz
500 ml	chicken stock (see box, page 57) or water	16 fl oz
10 ml	arrowroot	2 tsp
15 ml	water	1 tbsp

1 TIE UP THE BIRDS

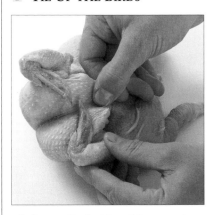

1 Season the insides of the poussins with salt and pepper. Hold one bird, breast-side down, on a work surface, tuck the neck skin under the bird, and cover with the wings.

2 Turn the bird over and pass a length of string under the tail end of the bird; tie a secure knot over the leg joints.

ANNE SAYS
"Poussins hold their shape and cook evenly when they are tied up."

Use white kitchen string for tying

Cross ends of legs so they can be tied together easily

Keep string pulled taut while tying up poussin

3 Bring the strings along the sides of the body, between the breast and the legs of the poussin, and loop them around the legs.

4 Turn the bird over so that it is breast-side down again and tie the strings tightly under the body.

5 Bring both ends of the string down between the sides of the body and the insides of the wings.

6 Tie the wing bones at the neck opening so they are tucked securely under the body. Repeat the whole process with the remaining poussins and set aside.

2 BLANCH THE CABBAGE

1 With the chef's knife, trim off the stalk end from the cabbage. Pull away the dark outer leaves and discard them.

Discard dark leaves as they may be bitter

2 Cut the cabbage lengthwise in half. Set each half flat-side down on the chopping board and cut it into quarters.

3 Rest the stalk end of each quarter on the chopping board and cut out the core. Coarsely shred each quarter of cabbage and discard any tough ribs.

4 Fill the large pan with salted water and bring to a boil. Add the cabbage, return the water to a boil, and simmer, 2 minutes. Drain the cabbage thoroughly in the colander.

3 ASSEMBLE AND BAKE THE DISH

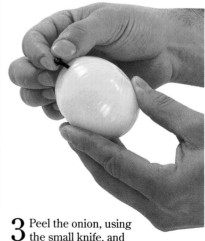

1 With the small knife, cut the plums in half using the indentation on one side as a guide. Scoop out the stones with the knife and discard them.

2 Heat the oven to 180°C (350°F, Gas 4). Stack the bacon rashers on the chopping board and cut crosswise into 1.25 cm (¹/₂ inch) strips.

3 Peel the onion, using the small knife, and stud it with the clove.

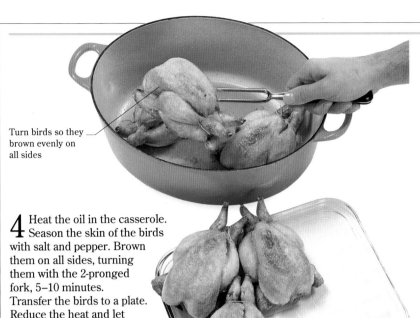

Turn birds so they brown evenly on all sides

4 Heat the oil in the casserole. Season the skin of the birds with salt and pepper. Brown them on all sides, turning them with the 2-pronged fork, 5–10 minutes. Transfer the birds to a plate. Reduce the heat and let the casserole cool slightly.

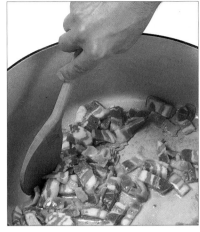

5 Add the bacon to the casserole and cook, stirring occasionally, until the fat is rendered (melted), 3–5 minutes.

CHICKEN STOCK

Chicken stock is an indispensable ingredient in many sauces and stews. It keeps well, up to 3 days, covered, in the refrigerator, and it also freezes well. Stock is often reduced to concentrate the flavour for a recipe, so salt and pepper are not added while it is cooking.

🍴 MAKES 2 LITRES (3¼ PINTS)

🥄 WORK TIME 15 MINUTES

🍲 COOKING TIME UP TO 3 HOURS

SHOPPING LIST

1	stewing chicken	1
1	onion	1
1	carrot	1
1	celery stick	1
1	bouquet garni, made with 5–6 parsley stalks, 2–3 sprigs of fresh thyme, and 1 bay leaf	1
2.5–5 ml	peppercorns	½–1 tsp
2 litres	water, more if needed	3¼ pints

1 Put the chicken in a large pan. Peel and quarter the onion and carrot; quarter the celery. Add to the pan with the bouquet garni and peppercorns.

2 Add water just to cover the ingredients. Bring to a boil and simmer, 1¼–1½ hours, skimming the stock occasionally.

3 Remove the stewing chicken from the pan of stock once the thighs are tender when pierced with a skewer. Continue simmering the stock, about 1½ hours longer.

Strain to remove flavouring ingredients

4 Using a ladle, strain the stock into a large bowl.

6 Spoon off all but 30 ml (2 tbsp) of fat. Stir in half of the cabbage, with a little salt and pepper, and spread it evenly in the casserole. Add the browned poussins, and arrange two-thirds of the plum halves over them.

HOW TO MAKE A BOUQUET GARNI

This bundle of aromatic herbs is designed to be easily lifted, and discarded at the end of cooking.

To make a bouquet garni, hold 2–3 sprigs of fresh thyme, 1 bay leaf, and 5–6 parsley stalks together, in your hand, in a bundle. Wind a piece of string around the herbs a few times and tie securely.

Blanched cabbage covers poussins and helps keep them moist

Stock will form rich sauce with flavours from poussins, plums, and vegetables

Plums add fruity flavour to sauce

7 Add the clove-studded onion and bouquet garni. Cover with the remaining cabbage, and pour over the wine and stock. Cover, transfer to the oven, and bake until the birds are cooked and the juices run clear when the thighs are pierced with the 2-pronged fork, 45–55 minutes.

! TAKE CARE !
Be sure that the poussins are thoroughly cooked.

8 Discard the onion and bouquet garni. Transfer the birds to the chopping board; remove the strings. Taste the cabbage mixture for seasoning.

Birds sit neatly on top of cabbage

Foil keeps birds warm and moist while dish is finished

9 With the slotted spoon, transfer the cabbage mixture to a warmed large serving dish. Set the birds on top, cover the dish with foil, and keep warm.

4 FINISH THE DISH

Plums should still hold their shape after simmering

1 Add the remaining plums to the cooking liquid and simmer until they are just tender, 5–8 minutes. Lift them out with the slotted spoon and arrange them with the poussins and cabbage in the centre of the dish.

2 Boil the liquid until well flavoured and reduced by about half, 5–10 minutes. Stir the arrowroot and water together to form a smooth paste. Whisk enough of the paste into the liquid so it thickens to lightly coat the back of a spoon. Taste for seasoning.

¶◉¶ TO SERVE
Spoon some sauce over the poussins and serve the rest separately.

Poussin is ideal size for individual serving

POUSSINS WITH CARROTS AND CABBAGE
Here, golden carrots replace the purple plums for satisfying country fare.

1 Omit the plums. Tie up the poussins, then shred the Savoy cabbage, and blanch it, as directed.
2 Peel and trim 6 medium carrots (total weight about 500 g/1 lb); cut them into 5 cm (2 inch) lengths. Alternatively, trim the tops from 24 baby carrots, leaving about 1.25 cm (½ inch) of green. Scrape them with a small knife to remove the skin.
3 Brown the poussins, and cook the bacon as directed. Mix half of the cabbage with the bacon in the casserole and season with salt and pepper. Top with the poussins and all of the carrots, followed by the remaining cabbage.
4 Bake the casserole and finish the sauce as directed. Serve the poussins with the carrots on a bed of cabbage on warmed plates.

Plums add unusual fruity flavour to braised cabbage with bacon

MALAYSIAN CHICKEN AND PRAWNS

Laksa Lemak

iOi SERVES 6 🥄 WORK TIME 35–40 MINUTES ♨ COOKING TIME 30–35 MINUTES

EQUIPMENT

bowls

food processor †

large pan

wok ‡

wok stirrer

slotted spoon

chef's knife

small knife

colander

chopping board

medium saucepan

† blender can also be used
‡ large frying pan can also be used

This popular combination of chicken and prawns has an Asian twist with coconut milk, ginger, and sweet spices; noodles and tofu add extra body.

GETTING AHEAD

The chicken can be poached 1 day ahead and kept in its poaching liquid, covered, in the refrigerator. The ingredients can be prepared up to 2 hours ahead and refrigerated. The dish should be cooked just before serving.

metric	SHOPPING LIST	imperial
750 g	skinless, boneless chicken breasts	1½ lb
750 ml	water	1¼ pints
	salt and pepper	
500 g	raw, unpeeled medium prawns	1 lb
3	garlic cloves	3
5 cm	piece of fresh root ginger	2 inch
6	shallots	6
3	dried red chillies, more to taste	3
7.5 ml	ground turmeric	1½ tsp
15 ml	ground coriander	1 tbsp
250 g	tofu	8 oz
250 g	bean sprouts	8 oz
1	small bunch of spring onions	1
125 g	thin rice noodles	4 oz
30 ml	vegetable oil	2 tbsp
500 ml	canned thick coconut milk	16 fl oz

INGREDIENTS

chicken breasts

raw, medium prawns

rice noodles †

tofu

vegetable oil

bean sprouts

coconut milk

garlic cloves

shallots

ground turmeric

fresh root ginger

dried red chillies

ground coriander

spring onions

† vermicelli noodles can also be used

ORDER OF WORK

1 POACH THE CHICKEN; PEEL THE PRAWNS

2 PREPARE THE STEW INGREDIENTS

3 ASSEMBLE THE DISH

1 POACH THE CHICKEN; PEEL THE PRAWNS

1 Separate the small piece of fillet meat from each chicken breast by pulling it off with your fingers. Strip the tendon from each fillet, stroking it with the small knife to remove it cleanly.

2 Bring the water to a boil in the saucepan; add the chicken breasts and fillets, salt, and pepper.

3 Simmer until the chicken is tender when pierced at the thickest portion and the juices run clear, 5–8 minutes for the fillets, 12–15 minutes for the breasts.

4 Meanwhile, peel off the prawn shells with your fingers and discard them. Make a shallow cut along the back of each of the peeled prawns, with the small knife, and remove the dark intestinal vein.

5 With the slotted spoon, transfer the chicken to the chopping board. Reserve the poaching liquid.

Cut chicken into bite-sized cubes

6 When the chicken is cool, halve each breast lengthwise, then crosswise into 2.5 cm (1 inch) pieces. Cut each fillet into 2–3 pieces.

Curl fingers under and guide knife with knuckles when cutting

HOW TO SOAK AND SEED DRIED RED CHILLIES

When handling hot chillies, avoid contact with your eyes. For a hotter flavour, add the seeds.

1 Put the dried chillies in a bowl and pour over enough hot water to cover. Leave to soften, about 5 minutes, then drain.

2 With a small knife, cut each of the soaked chillies lengthwise in half.

3 Holding the end of each chilli half, scrape out the core, seeds and white ribs from each half, using the small knife.

2 PREPARE THE STEW INGREDIENTS

1 Set the flat side of the chef's knife on each garlic clove and strike it with your fist. Discard the skin. Peel, slice, and crush the fresh root ginger (see box, page 64).

Use heavy knife to crush garlic slightly and loosen skin

2 Peel the shallots, separate them into sections, if necessary, and cut them into 2–3 pieces. Soak and seed the dried chillies (see box, left).

Root ginger is crushed before adding to food processor so it will be soft enough to purée

3 In the food processor, combine the shallots, garlic, chillies, ground turmeric, coriander, and crushed ginger slices; work the ingredients to a smooth paste.

ANNE SAYS
"If the mixture is very thick, add 2–3 spoonfuls of the chicken poaching liquid."

4 Drain the tofu in the colander and discard the liquid. On the chopping board, cut it into 1.25 cm (¹/₂ inch) slices using the chef's knife.

5 Stack the slices and cut them into 1.25 cm (¹/₂ inch) strips. Gather the strips together into a pile with your fingers, and cut crosswise into 1.25 cm (¹/₂ inch) cubes.

Fresh bean sprouts should be crisp

6 Pick over the bean sprouts and discard any that are brown. Trim the spring onions and cut them into thick diagonal slices, including some of their green tops.

Cut spring onions diagonally to make more attractive

Long thread-like rice noodles are very brittle before soaking

Rice noodles need only be soaked in boiling water

7 Fill the large pan with salted water and bring to a boil. Add the rice noodles and remove the pan from the heat. Allow the noodles to soften until they are tender but still slightly chewy, 3–5 minutes, or according to package directions. Gently stir them occasionally to prevent them sticking to each other.

8 Drain the noodles in the colander, rinse under hot water, and drain again thoroughly.

HOW TO PEEL, SLICE, AND CRUSH FRESH ROOT GINGER

Fresh root ginger must be crushed to release its flavour throughout a dish. The crushed slices can then be chopped or puréed, if needed.

1 With a small knife, carefully peel the skin from the piece of fresh root ginger and discard it.

2 Using a chef's knife, slice the ginger, cutting across the fibrous grain.

3 Place the flat side of the chef's knife on the slices of ginger and crush them by pressing firmly on the blade with your fist.

3 ASSEMBLE THE DISH

1 Heat the oil in the wok. Add the puréed ingredients, and cook gently, stirring constantly, until fragrant, 1–2 minutes.

ANNE SAYS
"The stirrer for the wok has a curved edge so it stays in constant contact with the wok surface."

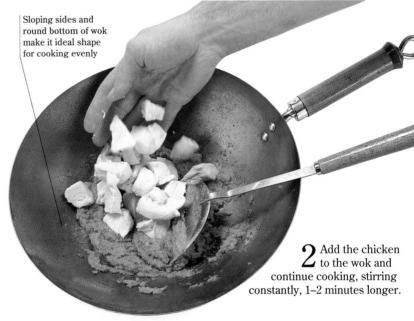

Sloping sides and round bottom of wok make it ideal shape for cooking evenly

2 Add the chicken to the wok and continue cooking, stirring constantly, 1–2 minutes longer.

3 Stir in the reserved poaching liquid and simmer until the mixture is rich and thickened, 20–25 minutes.

4 Add the prawns and simmer, stirring occasionally, until they begin to lose their transparency and turn pink, 3–5 minutes.

5 Add the tofu, bean sprouts, and noodles. Pour in the coconut milk and stir to combine. Simmer very gently, about 5 minutes longer. Stir in half of the spring onions. Taste the stew for seasoning.

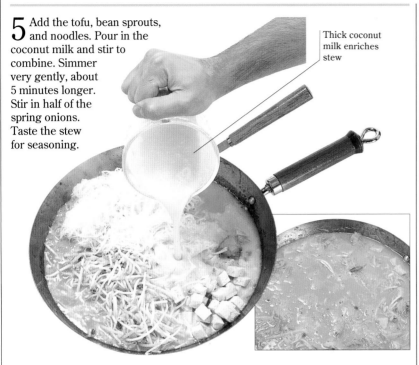

Thick coconut milk enriches stew

🍽 **TO SERVE**
Divide the stew between individual bowls and sprinkle with the remaining spring onions.

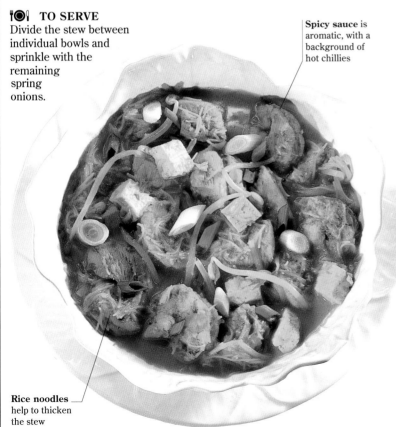

Spicy sauce is aromatic, with a background of hot chillies

Rice noodles help to thicken the stew

V A R I A T I O N

THAI CHICKEN AND PRAWNS

Thailand has an equally exotic stew, featuring lemon grass and fresh coriander.

1 Omit the dried red chillies, water, ground turmeric, ground coriander, bean sprouts, and tofu. Finely chop the leaves from 1 large bunch of fresh coriander, reserving half of the stalks.
2 Chop 2 stalks of lemon grass or grate the zest from 2 lemons. Peel 3 shallots. Prepare a 1.25 cm (1 inch) piece of fresh root ginger as directed.
3 In a food processor or blender, combine the garlic, lemon grass or lemon zest, ginger, shallots, and the reserved coriander stalks. Work the ingredients to form a smooth paste.
4 Cut the chicken breasts crosswise into the thinnest possible slices.
5 Core, halve, and seed 2 fresh red chillies. Slice thinly, then cut into fine dice. Prepare the noodles as directed.
6 Squeeze the juice from 2 limes; you should have 75 ml (2½ fl oz) juice.
7 Heat the oil in a wok and cook the puréed ingredients as directed. Add the chicken, prawns, salt, and pepper; stir-fry until the chicken and prawns are cooked, 3–5 minutes.
8 Stir in 500 ml (16 fl oz) each coconut milk and chicken stock or water, the lime juice, and 60 ml (2 fl oz) Asian fish sauce (nam pla or patis). Simmer, 2 minutes, then add the chopped chillies and coriander.
9 Stir in the noodles and simmer just until tender, 3–5 minutes. Taste for seasoning and serve in warmed bowls.

DUCK WITH TURNIPS AND APRICOTS

🍽️ SERVES 4   🥣 WORK TIME 35–40 MINUTES   🍲 COOKING TIME 1½–2 HOURS

EQUIPMENT

bowls

large frying pan

poultry shears†

boning knife

chef's knife

2-pronged fork

small knife

wooden spoon

vegetable peeler

large flameproof casserole, with lid

chopping board

† chef's knife can also be used

This rustic preparation of duck combines turnips and apricots with Madeira wine to add the traditional touch of sweetness to the stew. Wide egg noodles are a perfect accompaniment.

GETTING AHEAD

The duck stew can be made up to 1 day ahead and kept, covered, in the refrigerator; the flavours will mellow. Gently reheat the stew on top of the stove.

metric	SHOPPING LIST	imperial
1	duck, weighing about 1.8 kg (4 lb)	1
12–16	pickling onions	12–16
500 g	turnips	1 lb
2	shallots	2
	salt and pepper	
15 ml	vegetable oil	1 tbsp
15 g	butter	½ oz
30 ml	plain flour	2 tbsp
175 ml	dry white wine	6 fl oz
500 ml	brown veal stock (see box, page 109), more if needed	16 fl oz
1	bouquet garni, made with 5–6 parsley stalks, 2–3 sprigs of fresh thyme, and 1 bay leaf	1
5 ml	granulated sugar	1 tsp
175 g	stoned dried apricots	6 oz
60 ml	Madeira wine	4 tbsp

INGREDIENTS

duck

stoned dried apricots

plain flour

shallots

sugar

pickling onions

turnips

dry white wine

Madeira wine

vegetable oil

veal stock †

bouquet garni

butter

† water can also be used

ORDER OF WORK

1 JOINT THE DUCK

2 PREPARE THE VEGETABLES

3 COOK THE STEW

1 JOINT THE DUCK

1 Trim the excess fat and skin from the duck. Using the boning knife, cut down between one leg and the body of the duck. Twist the leg sharply outwards to break the joint, cut through it, and cut the whole leg from the body. Repeat with the other leg.

Sharp knife cuts easily between duck leg and body

2 Cut each leg in half at the joint between the thigh and the drumstick, using the line of white fat on the underside as a guide.

3 Slit closely along both sides of the breastbone to loosen the skin and meat from the bone. With the poultry shears or the chef's knife, cut along the breastbone to split it lengthwise in half.

4 Turn the bird over and cut away the rib bones and backbone in one piece, from the breast, leaving the breast pieces with the wing joints attached. Discard the back and rib bones.

5 Cut each breast piece diagonally in half, cutting through the breast and rib bones so that a portion of the breast meat is left with the wing joint. Cut off any sharp bones.

ANNE SAYS
"You can ask your butcher to joint the duck for you, but the backbone may be included."

Cut breast into 2 equal pieces to cook evenly

2 PREPARE THE VEGETABLES

1 Put the pickling onions in a bowl, cover with boiling water, and let stand, 2 minutes. Peel them, leaving a little of the root attached.

2 Trim off the ends of the turnips and peel them using the vegetable peeler. Cut small turnips into quarters and large ones into eighths. With the small knife, trim off the sharp edges so they are rounded.

3 Peel the shallots, leaving a little of the root attached; separate them into sections, if necessary. Slice them horizontally, then vertically, towards the root, leaving the slices attached at the root. Cut across into fine dice.

3 COOK THE STEW

1 Heat the oven to 180°C (350°F, Gas 4). Season the duck with salt and pepper. Heat the oil and butter in the casserole and add the duck, skin-side down. Brown well over low heat, 20–25 minutes. Turn the pieces and brown the other sides more quickly, about 5 minutes. Transfer to a plate and set aside.

Pan should not be crowded when browning duck pieces

ANNE SAYS

"The duck should be well browned so that the fat under the skin is thoroughly melted."

2 Transfer all but 30–45 ml (2–3 tbsp) fat from the casserole to the frying pan. Return the casserole to the heat. Add the flour and cook, stirring constantly with the wooden spoon, until the mixture is lightly browned but not burnt, 1–2 minutes.

3 Add the white wine, stock, bouquet garni, salt, pepper, and chopped shallots to the casserole. Bring the mixture to a boil and add the duck pieces. Cover, and cook in the heated oven, 40–45 minutes.

4 Meanwhile, heat the duck fat in the frying pan. Add the onions, turnips, sugar, salt, and pepper; cook, shaking the frying pan occasionally, until all the vegetables are evenly browned, 5–7 minutes.

5 Remove the stew from the oven; add the onions, turnips, and apricots. Stir in more stock if the sauce is very thick and the ingredients are not covered.

ANNE SAYS
"The dried apricots will plump and soften when cooked in the stew."

Add apricots and vegetables towards end of cooking so they will not overcook

Sauce is rich in flavour from veal stock

6 Cover and continue cooking in the oven until the duck and vegetables are tender, 20–25 minutes longer. Skim off any fat from the surface. Stir in the Madeira wine, bring just to a boil on top of the stove, taste for seasoning, and adjust if needed.

Delicate chervil leaves add a splash of colour to noodles

¶◎¶ TO SERVE
Serve the duck stew on warmed individual plates, on a bed of wide egg noodles, if you like.

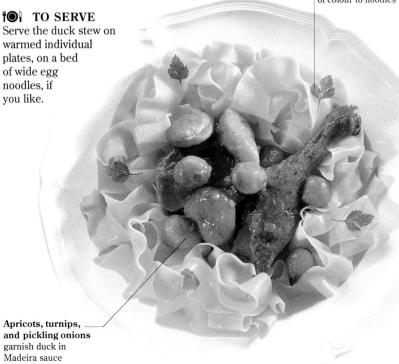

Apricots, turnips, and pickling onions garnish duck in Madeira sauce

V A R I A T I O N

DUCK WITH FRESH FIGS AND PORT

Fresh figs replace the turnips and apricots in this duck stew, while port adds rich colour and sweetness.

1 Omit the turnips, dried apricots, white wine, and Madeira. Cut up the duck, and prepare the shallots and pickling onions as directed.
2 Cook the duck as directed, adding 175 ml (6 fl oz) port with the veal stock, chopped shallots, bouquet garni, salt, and pepper.

3 Meanwhile, trim the stalks from 500 g (1 lb) fresh figs and halve the figs with a small knife.
4 Brown the onions as directed, add them to the stew, and cook, 5–10 minutes. Add the figs and cook the stew, 5–10 minutes longer. When the duck is tender, stir in 60 ml (4 tbsp) more port and bring back to a boil. Taste for seasoning and serve, decorated with thyme leaves, if you like.

INDIAN LAMB CURRY

Dhansak

 SERVES 6 WORK TIME 40–45 MINUTES COOKING TIME 1½–1¾ HOURS

EQUIPMENT

bowls

colander

chef's knife

wooden spoon

paper towels

slotted spoon

small knife

large flameproof casserole, with lid

chopping board

This spicy lamb curry is traditionally made with no less than three different types of lentils and an abundance of vegetables. My simple version is based on lamb with garam masala *(a spice mixture)*, simmered with aubergine, cauliflower, and a single kind of lentil. Fresh mango relish is an optional, colourful accompaniment.

GETTING AHEAD

The curry can be cooked 1–2 days ahead and kept, covered, in the refrigerator. Reheat it on top of the stove. The mango relish should be prepared no more than 2 hours ahead.

INGREDIENTS

boned shoulder of lamb

cauliflower

green lentils†

aubergine

garlic cloves

plain flour

onion

ground coriander

ground cumin

vegetable oil

cayenne pepper

ground turmeric

fresh root ginger

†brown or orange lentils can also be used

metric	SHOPPING LIST	imperial
1	large aubergine, weighing about 500 g (1 lb)	1
	salt and pepper	
1	small cauliflower, weighing about 750 g (1½ lb)	1
750 g	boned shoulder of lamb	1½ lb
5	garlic cloves	5
1	large onion	1
2 cm	piece of fresh root ginger	¾ inch
60 ml	vegetable oil	4 tbsp
15 ml	plain flour	1 tbsp
1.5 litres	water, more if needed	2⅓ pints
175 g	green lentils	6 oz
	mango relish (see box, page 72) for serving (optional)	
For the garam masala		
10 ml	each ground cumin, coriander, and turmeric	2 tsp
1	pinch of cayenne pepper	1

ORDER OF WORK

1 PREPARE THE INGREDIENTS

2 COOK THE LAMB CURRY

1 PREPARE THE INGREDIENTS

Cut aubergine into even-sized pieces

Leave skin on aubergine for more flavour

1 Trim and halve the aubergine lengthwise. Cut each half into 4–5 strips. Cut the strips across into 2.5 cm (1 inch) chunks. Put them in the colander; sprinkle generously with salt. Let stand to draw out bitter juices and soften slightly, 30 minutes.

2 Meanwhile, cut the cauliflower florets from the stalk and leaves, using the small knife. Put the florets in a bowl, cutting any of the large ones into halves or quarters.

3 Rinse the salt from the aubergine under cold running water and drain well. Pat dry with paper towels.

4 Trim off any fat and sinew from the lamb, using the chef's knife, then cut the lamb into 2.5 cm (1 inch) cubes.

5 Set the flat side of the chef's knife on top of each garlic clove and strike it with your fist. Discard the skin and finely chop the garlic.

7 Using the small knife, peel the skin from the fresh root ginger. With the chef's knife, slice the ginger, cutting across the fibrous grain. Crush each slice with the flat of the knife, then finely chop the slices.

6 Peel the onion and cut it lengthwise in half. Set each half cut-side down and slice horizontally, then vertically, towards the root, leaving the slices attached at the root end. Cut across the onion to make dice.

Ginger is sliced across grain to cut through fibres

MANGO RELISH

This relish can be made 1–2 hours ahead, and the flavours will mellow.

⚍🍽 MAKES 375 ML (12 FL OZ)

🥣 WORK TIME 10 MINUTES

SHOPPING LIST

1	dried red chilli	1
1	large mango, weighing about 500 g (1 lb)	1
7–10	sprigs of fresh coriander	7–10
5 mm	piece of fresh root ginger	¼ inch

1 Put the dried red chilli in a small bowl and cover with hot water. Let soften, 5 minutes, then drain. Cut the chilli lengthwise in half, discard the core, and scrape out the seeds.

2 Cut both of the chilli halves lengthwise into very thin strips, gather the strips together, and cut crosswise to produce very fine dice.

3 Cut the mango lengthwise into 2 pieces, slightly off-centre so the knife just misses the stone. Repeat on the other side, leaving a little flesh around the stone. Discard the stone.

4 With a small knife, slash the cut-side of one mango piece in a lattice, at 5 mm (¼ inch) intervals, just cutting through the flesh. Holding the mango flesh upwards, carefully push the peel with your thumbs to turn it inside out, opening out the cuts.

This neat method of cutting mango flesh is called "hedgehog"

Golden mango relish is flecked with red chilli and green coriander

5 Cut the cubes of mango away from the skin into a bowl. Repeat with the other mango piece. Strip the coriander leaves from the stalks and finely chop the leaves. Peel, slice, and finely chop the root ginger.

6 In a small bowl, combine the mango cubes, chilli, ginger, salt, pepper, and chopped coriander leaves, and stir until mixed. Taste the mango relish for seasoning, cover, and chill, 30 minutes.

2 COOK THE LAMB CURRY

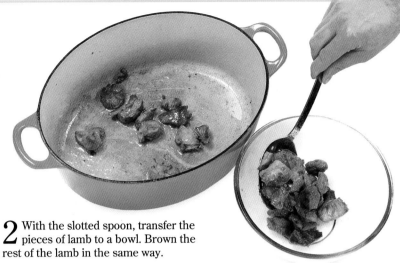

1 Heat two-thirds of the oil in the casserole. Add some of the lamb pieces to the casserole and season with salt and pepper. Cook over high heat, stirring occasionally, so the pieces brown evenly on all sides, 3–5 minutes.

2 With the slotted spoon, transfer the pieces of lamb to a bowl. Brown the rest of the lamb in the same way.

3 Add the remaining oil to the casserole, then add the aubergine, and cook, stirring occasionally, until brown, 5–7 minutes. With the slotted spoon, transfer to a separate bowl.

4 Add the onions to the casserole; cook, stirring occasionally, until golden brown, 7–10 minutes. Stir in the garlic and ginger; cook until softened and fragrant, 2–3 minutes longer.

5 Stir in the ground cumin, coriander, turmeric, and cayenne pepper; cook, stirring constantly, until thoroughly combined, 1–2 minutes.

! TAKE CARE !
Be sure to cook the spices very gently so they do not scorch.

Flour coats lamb pieces and thickens stew slightly

6 Return the lamb with any juices to the casserole. Sprinkle with the flour and cook, stirring until blended, about 1 minute.

Turmeric in garam masala
will colour cauliflower
vivid yellow

7 Stir in two-thirds of the water and
bring to a boil. Lower the heat,
cover, and simmer gently, stirring
occasionally, 30 minutes. Stir in the
lentils and cook, 15 minutes longer.

ANNE SAYS
*"Lentils will absorb a great deal of
liquid as they cook, so you may need
to add more water during cooking."*

8 Stir in the aubergine, cauliflower,
and the remaining water; continue
simmering, stirring often, until the
lamb is tender and the lentils and
vegetables are soft, 50–60 minutes.
Add more water during cooking if
the curry seems dry.

¡©¡ TO SERVE
Taste the curry for seasoning, transfer
to a warmed platter, and garnish with
shredded coriander leaves, if you like.
Pass the mango relish separately.

Saffron rice looks colourful
in centre of curry; extra rice
can be served in separate
bowls for each diner

Mango relish flavoured
with dried chilli adds heat
and sweetness to curry

74

VARIATION
INDIAN CHICKEN CURRY

The same spices flavour chicken, chickpeas, and vegetables in this curry. Serve it with Cucumber and Tomato Raita – cooling relish that is traditionally served with hotter Indian dishes.

1 Omit the lamb, cauliflower, and lentils. Prepare the aubergine as directed. Peel, seed, and coarsely chop 500 g (1 lb) medium tomatoes.
2 Sprinkle 1 chicken, jointed into 8 pieces (weighing about 1.6 kg/ 3 ½ lb), with salt and pepper. Heat the oil in a large casserole, add the chicken, skin-side down, and brown well, 5–7 minutes. Turn and brown the other side, then transfer to a plate.
3 Brown the aubergine as directed. Drain a 500 g (1 lb) can of chickpeas.
4 Cook the curry as directed, adding the tomatoes and 1 litre (1 ⅔ pints) water. Return the chicken to the casserole and simmer, 20 minutes.
5 Add the aubergine and chickpeas, then continue cooking, until the chicken is tender when pierced with a 2-pronged fork, 15–20 minutes longer. Taste the curry for seasoning and transfer to a warmed serving dish. Serve with a bowl of raita (see box, below) and with some naan bread, if you like.

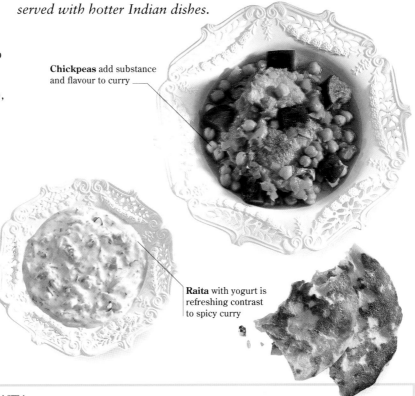

Chickpeas add substance and flavour to curry

Raita with yogurt is refreshing contrast to spicy curry

CUCUMBER AND TOMATO RAITA

🍽 MAKES 375 ML (12 FL OZ)

🥣 WORK TIME 15 MINUTES

SHOPPING LIST

1	small cucumber	1
1	small tomato	1
8	sprigs of fresh coriander	8
250 ml	plain yogurt	8 fl oz
	salt and pepper	

1 Coarsely grate cucumber, with its skin. Put it in a sieve set over a bowl. Squeeze it to remove as much juice as possible and transfer to a bowl. Peel, seed, and chop the tomato. Finely chop the coriander leaves.

2 Mix the cucumber with the tomato, coriander, and yogurt. Season to taste with salt and pepper.

LAMB CHOPS CHAMPVALLON

🍽 SERVES 6 🥄 WORK TIME 25–30 MINUTES ♨ BAKING TIME 2–2¼ HOURS

EQUIPMENT

2-pronged fork

chef's knife

vegetable peeler

large frying pan   pastry brush

wooden spoon

large metal spoon   pepper mill

23 x 32 cm (9 x13 inch) baking dish

large bowl

chopping board

This French dish of lamb chops baked between layers of sliced potatoes and onions dates back to the reign of Louis XIV. It is attributed to one of his mistresses who created it in an attempt to stay in the king's good graces. Despite its regal associations, this is a homely, peasant dish.

— GETTING AHEAD —

The casserole can be fully baked up to 1 day ahead and kept, covered, in the refrigerator; reheat it gently in a low oven.

INGREDIENTS

lamb loin chops   fresh thyme

beef stock   baking potatoes

garlic cloves   onions

black peppercorns

vegetable oil

ANNE SAYS
"Baking potatoes are high in starch and this will help to thicken the stock while the casserole is baking."

metric	SHOPPING LIST	imperial
500 g	onions	1 lb
1	small bunch of fresh thyme	1
3	garlic cloves	3
6	lamb loin chops, each 2.5 cm (1 inch) thick, total weight about 1 kg (2 lb)	6
	salt and freshly ground black pepper	
15 ml	vegetable oil, more for baking dish	1 tbsp
1.15 kg	baking potatoes	2½ lb
1 litre	beef or veal stock (see box, page 109), more if needed	1²/₃ pints

ORDER OF WORK

1 PREPARE THE INGREDIENTS

2 ASSEMBLE AND BAKE THE LAMB CHOPS

1 PREPARE THE INGREDIENTS

1 Peel the onions, leaving a little of the root attached, then cut them lengthwise in half. Lay each onion half flat on the chopping board and cut across into thin slices.

2 Strip the thyme leaves from the stalks, reserving a few sprigs for garnish. Peel and finely chop the garlic (see box, right).

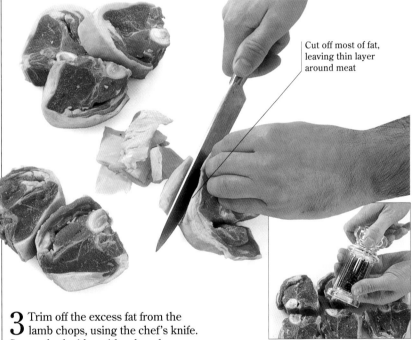

Cut off most of fat, leaving thin layer around meat

3 Trim off the excess fat from the lamb chops, using the chef's knife. Season both sides with salt and pepper.

4 Heat the oil in the large frying pan, add the chops, and cook over high heat until well browned, 1–2 minutes on each side.

ANNE SAYS
"The chops should only be browned on the outside at this point; cooking will continue in the oven."

HOW TO PEEL AND CHOP GARLIC

The strength of garlic varies with its age and dryness; use more when it is very fresh.

1 To separate the cloves, crush the bulb with the heel of your hand or pull a clove from the bulb with your fingers. To peel the clove, lightly crush it with the flat side of a chef's knife to loosen the skin.

2 Peel off the skin from the garlic clove with your fingers.

3 To crush the clove, set the flat side of the knife on top and strike firmly with your fist. Finely chop the garlic with the knife, moving the blade back and forth.

Browning seals
in juices and
adds flavour to
lamb chops

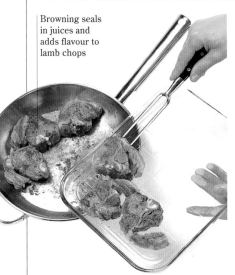

5 Remove the chops from the frying
pan with the 2-pronged fork.
Transfer to a plate and set aside.

6 Pour off all but about 15 ml
(1 tbsp) of fat from the pan.
Add the onions and cook over
medium heat, stirring, until soft
and translucent, 3–5 minutes.
Remove the pan from the heat.

! TAKE CARE !
*The onions should cook gently
without browning too much.*

Flavour from thyme
leaves infuses
vegetable mixture

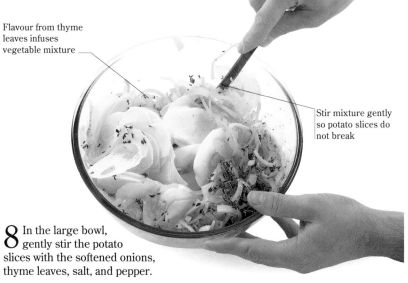

Stir mixture gently
so potato slices do
not break

7 Peel the potatoes. Cut a thin slice
from each potato so it sits flat on
the chopping board. Cut the potatoes
into very thin slices.

8 In the large bowl,
gently stir the potato
slices with the softened onions,
thyme leaves, salt, and pepper.

2 ASSEMBLE AND BAKE THE LAMB CHOPS

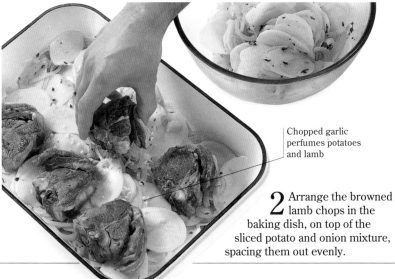

Chopped garlic
perfumes potatoes
and lamb

1 Heat the oven to 180°C (350°F,
Gas 4). Brush the baking dish with
oil. Spread half of the potato mixture in
an even layer in the dish. Sprinkle the
chopped garlic over the potatoes.

2 Arrange the browned
lamb chops in the
baking dish, on top of the
sliced potato and onion mixture,
spacing them out evenly.

3 Cover the lamb chops with the remaining potato mixture, arranging the potato slices neatly in rows. Pour over enough beef stock to come just to the top of the potatoes.

4 Transfer the dish to the heated oven and bake the casserole, uncovered, until the lamb chops and potatoes are tender when pierced with the 2-pronged fork, 2–2 1/4 hours.

ANNE SAYS
"The potatoes should be brown, and most of the liquid should have been absorbed. If the potatoes get dry before they are cooked, add more stock."

Beef stock almost covers potatoes to cook casserole evenly

¶◎¶ TO SERVE
Divide the chops, potatoes, and onions among 6 warmed plates and spoon over a little of the cooking liquid. Decorate with a sprig of thyme.

Glazed carrot sticks are a colourful accompaniment

Sliced potatoes should be crispy and brown

IRISH STEW
Leeks replace onions, creating this contemporary version of the famous Irish stew.

1 Omit the onions, garlic, and stock. Trim 750 g (1 1/2 lb) leeks, slit them lengthwise, and wash thoroughly. Cut into 1.25 cm (1/2 inch) slices, including some of the green.
2 Trim 6 lamb shoulder chops as directed. Slice 1 kg (2 lb) potatoes, then mix them with the thyme leaves, reserving a few leaves for garnish.
3 Brush a round casserole with oil. Spread half of the potatoes in the bottom of the casserole, followed by half of the sliced leeks; lightly season both layers with salt and pepper.
4 Season both sides of the lamb chops with salt and pepper and set them on top of the leeks. Add the remaining leeks, then potatoes, seasoning each layer with salt and pepper.
5 Pour over water to just cover the potatoes, cover the casserole, and bake until the chops and potatoes are tender when pierced with the 2-pronged fork, 1 1/4–1 1/2 hours.
6 Remove the lid from the casserole and continue baking until the potatoes are lightly browned, about 30–45 minutes longer. Sprinkle the stew with the reserved thyme leaves and serve directly from the casserole.

HAM BAKED WITH PRUNES IN RICH WINE SAUCE

🍲 SERVES 6   🥣 WORK TIME 40–45 MINUTES   🍲 BAKING TIME 20–25 MINUTES

EQUIPMENT

plastic bag

large gratin dish

chef's knife

pastry brush

bowls

rolling pin   small knife

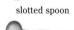

serrated knife

saucepans

wooden spoon

slotted spoon

ladle

whisk

chopping board

ANNE SAYS
"Use a heavy-based saucepan when making the syrup so the caramel does not burn."

I first tasted a version of this dish in the Chablis region of France, so white Chablis is the obvious wine to use, although any dry white will do. I've added prunes for natural sweetness and marc de Bourgogne *– a type of brandy that is distilled from grape crushings.*

GETTING AHEAD

The sauce can be made and the dish assembled up to 1 day ahead. Keep it, covered, in the refrigerator and bake it just before serving.

metric	SHOPPING LIST	imperial
135 g	stoned prunes	4¹/₂ oz
60 ml	marc de Bourgogne	4 tbsp
4	shallots	4
2.5 ml	black peppercorns	¹/₂ tsp
45 g	butter, more for gratin dish	1¹/₂ oz
30 ml	plain flour	2 tbsp
250 ml	dry white wine	8 fl oz
250 ml	beef stock (see box, page 109)	8 fl oz
	salt	
125 ml	double cream	4 fl oz
1 kg	piece of cooked ham	2 lb
For the vinegar and caramel syrup		
100 g	caster sugar	3 ¹/₄ oz
125 ml	water	4 fl oz
125 ml	red wine vinegar	4 fl oz

INGREDIENTS

shallots   cooked ham

double cream   butter   stoned prunes

caster sugar

beef stock

black peppercorns   red wine vinegar   marc †

plain flour

dry white wine

†brandy can also be used

ORDER OF WORK

1 MAKE THE VINEGAR AND CARAMEL SYRUP

2 PREPARE THE SAUCE

3 CARVE THE HAM AND FINISH THE DISH

1 MAKE THE VINEGAR AND CARAMEL SYRUP

3 Slowly add the vinegar. Simmer, stirring occasionally, to dissolve the caramel and reduce by half, 5–8 minutes. Remove from the heat.

! TAKE CARE !
The caramel splutters when the vinegar is added and the fumes will be strong; stand at arm's length when pouring.

1 Gently heat the sugar and water in a heavy-based saucepan until the sugar dissolves. Increase the heat and boil, without stirring, until the syrup starts to turn golden around the edge.

2 Reduce the heat and cook until the syrup becomes a deep golden caramel. Remove the saucepan from the heat and let the bubbles subside.

2 PREPARE THE SAUCE

1 Halve the prunes, using the small knife, and put them in a small saucepan with the marc.

Stoned prunes are easy to cut in half

Dark-coloured prunes will give sauce rich brown hue

2 Heat gently until the prunes are plump, 5–8 minutes. Using the slotted spoon, transfer the prunes to a plate; reserve the liquid.

3 Peel the outer, papery skin from the shallots using the small knife. Finely chop them (see box, page 82).

4 Put the peppercorns in the plastic bag. Hold the end of the bag closed and crush them gently with the rolling pin.

Plastic bag holds peppercorns conveniently for crushing

HOW TO CHOP A SHALLOT

For a standard chop, make slices that are about 3 mm (¹/₈ inch) thick. For a fine chop, slice the shallot as thinly as possible.

1 If necessary, separate the shallot into sections at the root and peel each section. Set each section, flat-side down, on a chopping board. Holding the shallot steady with your fingers, slice it horizontally towards the root using a chef's knife, leaving the slices attached at the root end.

2 Slice vertically through the shallot, again leaving the root end uncut.

3 Cut across the shallot to make fine dice. Continue chopping, if necessary, until very fine.

5 Melt the butter in a medium saucepan. Add the chopped shallots and cook, stirring occasionally, until softened but not browned, 3–5 minutes. Stir in the flour and cook until foaming, 30–60 seconds. Remove the saucepan from the heat and let cool slightly.

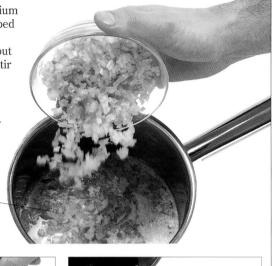

Shallots soften quickly in hot butter

6 Whisk in the white wine, return to the heat, and simmer, 1 minute. Add stock, prune soaking liquid, crushed peppercorns, and salt. Simmer, whisking constantly, until the sauce thickens and lightly coats the back of a spoon, 10–12 minutes.

7 Whisk the vinegar and caramel syrup into the sauce and continue simmering until it is again thick enough to coat the back of a spoon, 5–10 minutes longer.

Cream lightens colour of sauce and mellows flavour

8 Stir in the double cream. Reserving a few prunes for garnish, add the remainder to the pan and taste the sauce for seasoning.

ANNE SAYS
"Cooked ham is often salty, so additional salt may not be needed."

3 CARVE THE HAM AND FINISH THE DISH

1 Heat the oven to 180°C (350°F, Gas 4). Brush the gratin dish with melted butter. Holding the piece of ham steady with one hand, cut it across into 6 equal slices using the serrated knife.

ANNE SAYS
"Mark out even portions on the ham before you start slicing."

Boneless cooked ham is easy to slice

2 Arrange the ham slices evenly in the gratin dish, overlapping them slightly. Ladle over the sauce so the ham slices are completely coated. Bake the ham in the heated oven until hot and bubbling, 20–25 minutes.

Sauce is piquant with peppercorns, white wine, and a sweet-sour syrup of vinegar and caramel

🍽 TO SERVE
Garnish the ham with the reserved prune halves and serve directly from the gratin dish with parsley potatoes, if you like.

Sweet prunes are delicious with salty baked ham

HAM WITH WHITE WINE AND APPLES

Apples flamed in Calvados add Norman flavour to this version of baked ham.

1 Omit the prunes and marc. Make the sauce as directed, omitting the vinegar and caramel mixture; set aside.
2 Core 4 apples using an apple corer. Cut 2 apples crosswise into 1 cm (³/₈ inch) slices. Peel the remainder and cut them into dice.
3 Melt 15 g (¹/₂ oz) butter in a frying pan. Add half of the apple slices, sprinkle with 15 ml (1 tbsp) sugar, turn, and sprinkle with 15 ml (1 tbsp) more sugar. Fry until caramelized, 2–3 minutes on each side, and reserve. Repeat with the remaining slices.
4 Melt 30 g (1oz) more butter in the pan. Sauté the diced apples with 30 ml (2 tbsp) sugar, salt, and pepper until tender, 5–7 minutes.
5 Add 60 ml (2 fl oz) Calvados or brandy and bring to a boil. Flame the apples with a lighted match to set the alcohol alight. Shake the pan until the flames subside, 20–30 seconds.
6 Add the sauce to the diced apples and bring to a boil. Stir in the double cream, and taste for seasoning.
7 Bake the ham and sauce in the oven as directed. Serve with apple slices, and with sautéed fresh spinach, if you like.

BEEF, BARLEY, AND MUSHROOM STEW

  SERVES 6–8 🥣 WORK TIME 30–35 MINUTES ☕ COOKING TIME 2¼–2½ HOURS

EQUIPMENT

 2-pronged fork

bowls

kitchen string

small knife

chef's knife

vegetable peeler

paper towels

large flameproof casserole, with lid

wooden spoon

slotted spoon

chopping board

Barley is a tasty grain that is all too often overlooked. Here it adds body and a characteristic earthy taste to a hearty beef and mushroom stew. For a treat, I like to replace some of the common mushrooms with fresh wild mushrooms.

GETTING AHEAD

The stew can be made 1–2 days ahead and kept, covered, in the refrigerator. Reheat it gently on top of the stove, adding more stock or water if it has thickened on standing.

metric	SHOPPING LIST	imperial
1.4 kg	braising steak	3 lb
625 g	onions	1¼ lb
375 g	carrots	12 oz
500 g	mushrooms	1 lb
4	celery sticks	4
45 ml	vegetable oil	3 tbsp
	salt and pepper	
1	bouquet garni, made with 5–6 parsley stalks, 2–3 sprigs of fresh thyme, and 1 bay leaf	1
1 litre	beef stock (see box, page 109), more if needed	1⅔ pints
200 g	pearl barley	6½ oz

INGREDIENTS

braising steak   mushrooms

pearl barley

bouquet garni

celery sticks

carrots   onions

beef stock

vegetable oil

ANNE SAYS
"Pearl barley is the most common barley and needs no soaking before cooking."

ORDER OF WORK

1 PREPARE THE STEW INGREDIENTS

2 COOK THE STEW

1 PREPARE THE STEW INGREDIENTS

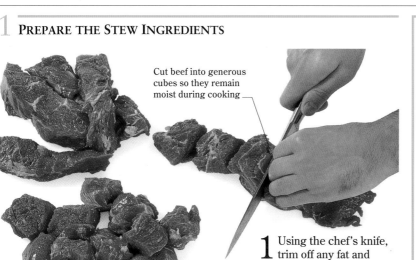

Cut beef into generous cubes so they remain moist during cooking

1 Using the chef's knife, trim off any fat and sinew from the beef and discard it. Cut the beef into thick slices, then cut crosswise into 5 cm (2 inch) cubes.

2 Peel the onions, leaving a little of the root attached, and cut them lengthwise in half. Lay each onion half flat on the chopping board and cut crosswise into thin slices.

3 Peel and trim off the ends of the carrots; if large, cut the carrots lengthwise in half. Cut them crosswise into 1.25 cm (½ inch) slices. Clean and slice the mushrooms (see box, right).

Celery is very easy to slice once strings have been removed

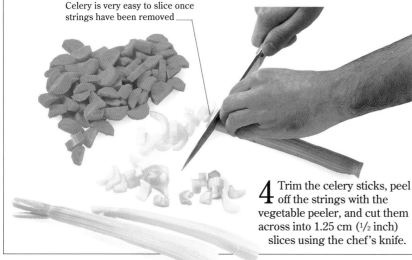

4 Trim the celery sticks, peel off the strings with the vegetable peeler, and cut them across into 1.25 cm (½ inch) slices using the chef's knife.

HOW TO CLEAN AND SLICE MUSHROOMS

Mushrooms absorb moisture quickly, so do not soak them in water. In order to cook evenly, mushrooms should be cut into equal-sized pieces.

1 Wipe the mushroom caps with damp paper towels.

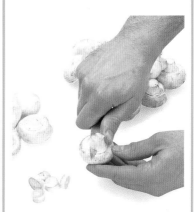

2 Trim the mushroom stalks even with the caps.

3 Set the mushrooms, stalk-side down, on a chopping board, and slice them vertically.

2 COOK THE STEW

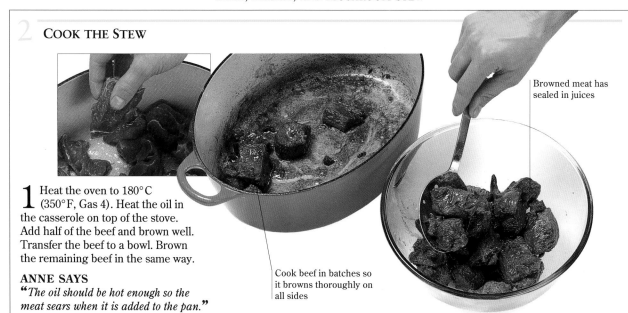

Browned meat has sealed in juices

Cook beef in batches so it browns thoroughly on all sides

1 Heat the oven to 180°C (350°F, Gas 4). Heat the oil in the casserole on top of the stove. Add half of the beef and brown well. Transfer the beef to a bowl. Brown the remaining beef in the same way.

ANNE SAYS
"The oil should be hot enough so the meat sears when it is added to the pan."

2 Add the sliced onions with a little salt and pepper to the casserole. Cook over medium heat, stirring, until lightly browned, 5–7 minutes.

3 Add the beef, bouquet garni, salt, and pepper to the casserole. Pour in the beef stock and stir to combine.

4 Cover the casserole with the lid and transfer to the heated oven. Cook the stew, stirring occasionally, about 1½ hours.

5 Add the carrots, celery, and barley to the stew. Stir in more stock or water, if necessary, to keep the casserole moist.

Barley cooks at same rate as vegetables

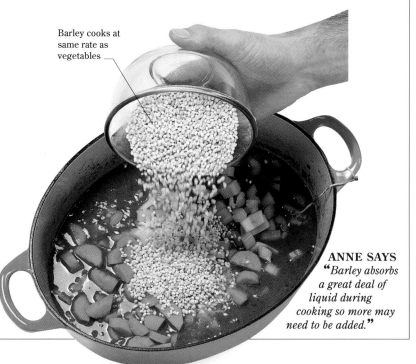

ANNE SAYS
"Barley absorbs a great deal of liquid during cooking so more may need to be added."

6 Cover and continue cooking until the meat and vegetables are tender when pierced with the 2-pronged fork, 40–45 minutes longer.

ANNE SAYS
"The barley should be tender but still slightly chewy."

7 About 10 minutes before the end of cooking, add the sliced mushrooms and stir to combine.

Mushrooms are added towards end of cooking so they do not overcook

¶◉¶ TO SERVE
Discard the bouquet garni and taste the stew for seasoning. Serve in warmed individual bowls, with crusty bread, if you like.

Barley makes this stew a substantial winter meal

Sauce should be well reduced, dark, and rich

V A R I A T I O N

BARLEY AND VEGETABLE STEW

A vegetable version of Beef, Barley, and Mushroom Stew. For a truly vegetarian dish, you can use vegetable stock instead of beef stock.

1 Omit the beef. Prepare the onions, 500 g (1 lb) carrots, 750 g (1½ lb) mushrooms, and 6 celery sticks as directed.
2 Cut the kernels from 4 fresh corn cobs: hold each cob vertically on a chopping board and cut from the tip down to the board with a chef's knife. Turn the cob, and continue removing as many whole kernels as possible. Alternatively, use 300 g (10 oz) defrosted sweetcorn kernels.
3 Heat the oil in a large casserole, and sauté the onions with salt and pepper, stirring, until brown, 5–7 minutes. Stir in the stock, barley, carrots, celery, and bouquet garni.
4 Cover, and cook in the oven as directed, stirring occasionally, until the barley and vegetables are almost tender, 40–45 minutes. Add the sweetcorn, mushrooms, and 125 g (4 oz) fresh or defrosted peas; continue cooking until the vegetables are tender, 10–15 minutes longer. Taste the stew for seasoning. Serve in warmed bowls.

PORTUGUESE PORK AND CLAM STEW

🍽 SERVES 6–8   🥄 WORK TIME 30–35 MINUTES*   🍲 COOKING TIME 2–2½ HOURS

EQUIPMENT

large flameproof casserole, with lid

saucepan

bowls

chef's knife

small knife

2-pronged fork

paper towels

whisk

wooden spoon

slotted spoon

chopping board

small stiff brush

The combination of rich pork with salty clams has been enjoyed on the Iberian peninsula for centuries. In Portugal, a lemon wedge is squeezed over each serving just before eating.

GETTING AHEAD
The pork can be cooked without the clams 1–2 days ahead and kept, covered, in the refrigerator. Gently reheat the stew and cook the clams just before serving.

*plus 24 hours marinating time

INGREDIENTS

boned loin of pork†

bay leaf

clams

parsley

tomato purée

paprika

tomatoes

lemon

olive oil

dry white wine

Tabasco sauce

garlic cloves

onion

†pork shoulder can also be used

metric	SHOPPING LIST	imperial
1.4 kg	boned loin of pork	3 lb
1 kg	hard-shell clams, such as amandes	2 lb
500 g	tomatoes	1 lb
2	garlic cloves	2
1	large onion	1
15 ml	tomato purée	1 tbsp
1	dash of Tabasco sauce, more to taste	1
1	lemon for serving	1
1	bunch of parsley for garnish	1
	For the marinade	
2	garlic cloves	2
1	bay leaf	1
22.5 ml	paprika	1½ tbsp
	salt and pepper	
45 ml	olive oil	3 tbsp
375 ml	dry white wine, more if needed	12 fl oz

ORDER OF WORK

1 MARINATE THE PORK

2 PREPARE THE STEW INGREDIENTS

3 FINISH THE STEW

1 MARINATE THE PORK

1 Trim off excess fat and sinew from the pork, using the chef's knife. Cut the meat lengthwise into thick strips, and then cut crosswise into 2.5 cm (1 inch) cubes.

Some fat can be left on pork to flavour stew

2 Set the flat side of the chef's knife on top of each of the garlic cloves and strike it with your fist. Discard the skins, and finely chop the garlic; transfer to a large non-metallic bowl.

3 With your fingers, crumble the bay leaf into the bowl with the garlic. Discard the central stem of the leaf.

4 Add the paprika, plenty of black pepper, 15 ml (1 tbsp) oil, and the white wine; whisk to combine thoroughly. Add the pork and mix well. Cover and marinate in the refrigerator, stirring occasionally, 24 hours.

Wine in marinade will add depth of flavour to stew

2 PREPARE THE STEW INGREDIENTS

1 Scrub the clams under cold water with the brush and discard any with broken shells or that do not close when tapped.

2 Core the tomatoes and score an "x" on each. Immerse in boiling water until the skins split, 8–15 seconds. Transfer to cold water. Peel, halve, and seed them; coarsely chop each half.

3 Peel and finely chop the garlic. Peel the onion, leaving a little of the root attached, then halve it lengthwise. Cut each half across into thin slices.

3 FINISH THE STEW

Paper towels absorb liquid so meat will brown evenly

1 Heat the oven to 180°C (350°F, Gas 4). Transfer the meat to a plate lined with paper towels using the slotted spoon; reserve the marinade. Dry the meat with paper towels.

2 Heat the remaining oil in the large casserole. Add the pork and brown well on all sides. With the slotted spoon, transfer the meat to a bowl.

ANNE SAYS
"Cook the meat in batches, if necessary, so that it browns thoroughly."

3 Lower the heat and add the onions and garlic, with a little salt and pepper. Cover the casserole and cook very gently, stirring occasionally with the wooden spoon, until the onions are very soft and brown, 20–25 minutes.

Marinade doubles as cooking liquid for stew

4 Add the chopped tomatoes, tomato purée, Tabasco sauce, and the pork to the casserole. Pour in the reserved marinade and stir well.

5 Cover, and cook in the oven until the pork is tender when pierced with the 2-pronged fork, stirring occasionally, 1½–1¾ hours. Add more wine if the stew becomes dry.

6 Meanwhile, trim the ends from the lemon and cut it lengthwise in half. Lay each half cut-side down and cut into 4 wedges.

7 Strip the parsley leaves from the stalks and pile the leaves on the chopping board. With the chef's knife, coarsely chop the leaves.

Clams are cooked by steam from stew

8 Arrange the clams on top of the pork, cover with the lid, and cook in the oven until the clams open, 15–20 minutes longer. Discard any clams that are still closed after cooking.

Salty clams are a delicious contrast to pork

🍴 **TO SERVE**

Transfer the stew to a warmed serving bowl. Sprinkle with chopped parsley. Serve the lemon wedges in a separate bowl.

Lemon is traditional accompaniment to pork and clam stew

CHILEAN PORK AND BEANS

To save time, you can use 625 g (1½ lb) canned red kidney beans instead of dried beans.

1 Omit the marinade and clams. Put 375 g (12 oz) dried red kidney beans in a bowl. Cover with water and let soak overnight. Drain and rinse.
2 Put the beans in a saucepan, cover with water, and boil, 10 minutes. Reduce the heat, cover, and simmer until almost tender but still slightly firm, ¾–1½ hours. Drain well.
3 Meanwhile, prepare the tomatoes, garlic, and onion as directed. Core, seed, and dice 1 fresh hot green chilli and 2 green peppers.
4 Peel 500 g (1 lb) each of yams and sweet potatoes; cut them into 2.5 cm (1 inch) cubes. Chop 7–10 sprigs each of parsley, coriander, and oregano.
5 Brown the pork; cook the onions and garlic as directed. Return the pork to the pan. Add the tomatoes, tomato purée, herbs, and 500 ml (16 fl oz) water. Cover, and cook until the pork is just tender, 1¼–1½ hours. Add the vegetables, beans, and 750 ml (1¼ pints) more water to cover.
6 Cook, stirring occasionally, until tender, 40–45 minutes longer. Transfer the stew to the stove, stir in 30 ml (2 tbsp) red wine vinegar, and simmer, uncovered, 5 minutes. Taste for seasoning and serve in warmed bowls.

FRENCH BEEF AND HERB POTATO PIE

Hachis Parmentier aux Herbes

  SERVES 6   WORK TIME 45–50 MINUTES   BAKING TIME 35–40 MINUTES

EQUIPMENT

bowls

food processor †

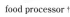
wooden spoon

pastry brush

slotted spoon

large sauté pan

large shallow
baking dish

colander   vegetable
peeler

saucepans, 1 with lid

metal skewer

rubber spatula

chef's knife

small knife

potato
masher

† blender can also be used

INGREDIENTS

parsley   basil

milk   minced
beef   dry white
wine

tomatoes   onion

olive oil

garlic cloves

beef stock †   potatoes

† water can also be used

A contemporary update of a French classic designed to use up the remains of a beef roast. This version uses fresh minced beef instead of leftover meat, with a topping of herb-flavoured potato purée.

GETTING AHEAD

The pie can be assembled up to 1 day ahead and kept, covered, in the refrigerator. It should be baked just before serving.

metric	SHOPPING LIST	imperial
1	large onion	1
375 g	tomatoes	12 oz
4	garlic cloves	4
75 ml	olive oil	2½ fl oz
1 kg	minced beef	2 lb
	salt and pepper	
250 ml	beef stock (see box, page 109)	8 fl oz
125 ml	dry white wine	4 fl oz
	For the herb potatoes	
1 kg	potatoes	2 lb
1	bunch of fresh basil	1
1	bunch of parsley	1
250 ml	milk, more if needed	8 fl oz

ORDER OF WORK

1 COOK THE
    MINCED BEEF

2 MAKE THE HERB
    MASHED POTATOES

3 ASSEMBLE AND
    BAKE THE PIE

1 COOK THE MINCED BEEF

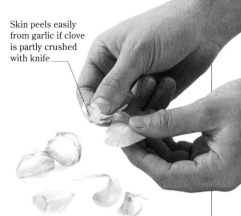

Skin peels easily
from garlic if clove
is partly crushed
with knife

1 Peel the onion, leaving a little of the root attached; cut it lengthwise in half. Lay each half flat on a chopping board and slice horizontally, then vertically, towards the root, leaving the slices attached at the root end. Finally, cut across to make dice.

2 Core the tomatoes and score an "x" in each. Immerse in boiling water until the skins start to split, 8–15 seconds, depending on their ripeness. Transfer to cold water. When cool, peel and halve them crosswise. Squeeze out the seeds and coarsely chop each half.

3 Set the flat side of the chef's knife on top of each garlic clove and strike it with your fist. Discard the skins and finely chop 2 of the cloves.

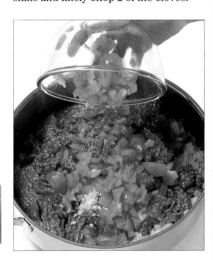

4 Heat one-third of the oil in the sauté pan or in a frying pan. Add the onion and cook, stirring, until soft but not brown, 3–5 minutes.

5 Add the chopped garlic, minced beef, salt, pepper, and chopped tomatoes. Lower the heat and cook very gently, stirring occasionally, until the meat is brown, 10–12 minutes.

6 Pour in the stock and white wine, and stir to combine. Continue simmering over very low heat, stirring occasionally, until most of the liquid has evaporated but the meat is still very moist, 25–30 minutes. Meanwhile, make the herb mashed potatoes (see page 94).

! TAKE CARE !
*Do not cook the beef too fast
or it will be tough and chewy.*

White wine adds
rich flavour to meat
mixture as alcohol
evaporates

2 MAKE THE HERB MASHED POTATOES

1 Peel the skin from the potatoes and cut each one into 2–3 pieces, depending on their size.

Vegetable peeler removes only very thin layer of flesh beneath skin

Hold potato firmly while peeling

2 Put them in a saucepan with plenty of cold water and add salt. Cover and bring to a boil. Simmer until tender when pierced with the tip of the small knife, 15–20 minutes.

3 Meanwhile, strip the basil and parsley leaves from the stalks. Put the leaves and the 2 whole garlic cloves in the food processor.

4 Work the herbs and garlic with the remaining oil to form a purée, scraping the side of the bowl occasionally.

ANNE SAYS
"If the purée sticks to the side of the processor, push it down with the rubber spatula and add 3–4 spoonfuls of the milk."

5 Drain the potatoes and return them to the saucepan. Mash them with the potato masher. Add the herb purée to the potatoes.

6 Scald the milk in another saucepan. Gradually beat the milk into the potatoes over medium heat, and continue cooking and stirring until the potatoes just hold a shape, 2–3 minutes. Season to taste.

Stirring hot milk into potatoes lightens their texture

3 ASSEMBLE AND BAKE THE PIE

1 Heat the oven to 190°C (375°F, Gas 5). Brush the baking dish with oil. Taste the meat for seasoning, then spoon it, with any liquid, into the baking dish in an even layer. Cover with the herb potatoes and smooth the top with the back of a spoon.

2 Make a scalloped pattern on the herb potatoes with the tip of a dessert spoon. Dip the spoon in a bowl of water occasionally so the potato does not stick to it.

Scalloped edges have golden crests

3 Transfer the pie to the heated oven and bake until the top is golden brown and the skewer inserted in the centre for 30 seconds is hot to the touch, 35–40 minutes.

🍽 TO SERVE
Cut the pie into 6 portions and transfer to warmed individual plates.

Minced beef makes tasty filling

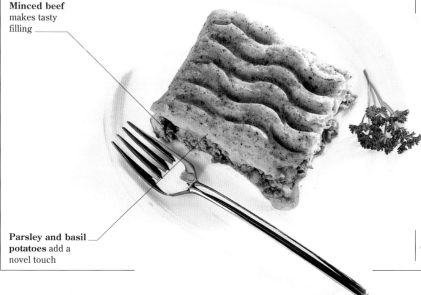

Parsley and basil potatoes add a novel touch

VARIATION

OLD EMILY'S SHEPHERD'S PIE

I was brought up on shepherd's pie made by our stout old housekeeper, Emily. She made it with leftover lamb or beef, but I like to use fresh minced lamb.

1 Omit the beef, wine, garlic, basil, parsley, olive oil, and tomatoes. Peel and trim 2 carrots, square off the sides, and cut vertically into 5 mm (¼ inch) slices. Cut into 5 mm (¼ inch) strips then cut crosswise into cubes.
2 Heat 15 ml (1 tbsp) vegetable oil in a large sauté pan or frying pan; sauté the carrots and onions until soft, 3–5 minutes; lower the heat to cool the pan.
3 Brown 1 kg (2 lb) minced lamb very gently. Add 250 ml (8 fl oz) beef stock or water, with 1 sprig each fresh thyme and rosemary; simmer as directed.
4 Discard the herbs and taste the lamb mixture for seasoning.
5 Meanwhile, peel and cook 1 kg (2 lb) potatoes as directed. Drain them and return them to the saucepan; mash them and stir in 45 g (1½ oz) butter. Beat in the hot milk as directed. Season to taste with salt and pepper.
6 Brush 6 individual heatproof bowls with melted butter and fill them with the lamb mixture. Divide the mashed potatoes among the bowls and make a design on the top with a fork. Bake in the oven as directed until golden brown.

PEPPERY TUSCAN BEEF STEW

Stracotto di Manzo Peposo

🍽️ SERVES 6 🥄 WORK TIME 35–40 MINUTES* 🍲 COOKING TIME 2–2½ HOURS

EQUIPMENT

bowls

chef's knife

small knife

pastry brush

slotted spoon

large metal spoon

paper towels

chopping board

large pan

wire rack

baking sheet

saucepan

ladle

wooden spoon

serrated knife

Italian cuisine at its simple best. There is more than a dash of pepper in this hearty stew of beef with red wine, pancetta, tomatoes, and garlic. Chianti is the wine of Tuscany but you can use any full-bodied red wine. Sage-flavoured fettunta– *rustic bread croûtes– are served alongside.*

GETTING AHEAD

The stew can be prepared up to 2 days ahead and kept, covered, in the refrigerator; the flavours will mellow. Gently reheat it on top of the stove and make the *fettunta* just before serving.

*plus 8–12 hours marinating time

INGREDIENTS

braising steak

pancetta †

garlic

Italian bread

plum tomatoes

onion

beef stock ‡

black pepper

bay leaves

red wine

fresh sage

olive oil

† bacon rashers can also be used
‡ water can also be used

ORDER OF WORK

1 PREPARE THE SAGE OIL; MARINATE THE BEEF

2 PREPARE THE VEGETABLES AND COOK THE STEW

3 MAKE THE SAGE-FLAVOURED FETTUNTA

metric	SHOPPING LIST	imperial
5–6	sprigs of fresh sage	5–6
30 ml	freshly ground black pepper	2 tbsp
300 ml	olive oil	½ pint
1.4 kg	braising steak	3 lb
500 g	plum or medium tomatoes	1 lb
1	large onion	1
6	garlic cloves	6
125 g	sliced pancetta	4 oz
2	bay leaves	2
250 ml	beef stock (see box, page 109), more if needed	8 fl oz
500 ml	red wine	16 fl oz
	salt	
500 g	loaf crusty Italian peasant-style bread	1 lb

1 PREPARE THE SAGE OIL; MARINATE THE BEEF

1 Chop the leaves from 2 of the sage sprigs (see box, below) and put them in a small bowl. In a large bowl, combine half of the black pepper with all but 45 ml (3 tbsp) of the oil. Ladle one-quarter of this mixture into the bowl with the chopped sage and set it aside for making the fettunta.

Some seasoned oil is reserved to brush on bread for fettunta

Chopped sage leaves will impart flavour to olive oil

2 Trim any fat and sinew from the beef. Using the chef's knife, cut the beef into 5 cm (2 inch) cubes.

Stir meat to moisten well with flavoured oil

3 Add the beef to the bowl with the black pepper and oil mixture. Stir until the beef is well coated with the oil. Cover, and leave to marinate in the refrigerator, stirring occasionally, 8–12 hours.

HOW TO CHOP HERBS

Sage, rosemary, parsley, dill, tarragon, and basil are herbs that are often chopped before being added to other ingredients. Do not chop delicate herbs like basil and tarragon too finely because they bruise easily.

1 Strip the leaves or sprigs from the stalks. Pile the leaves or sprigs on a chopping board.

Leaves are pulled from woody stalks

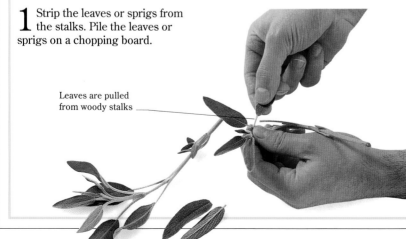

2 Cut the leaves or sprigs into pieces with a chef's knife and chop the herbs, rocking the knife back and forth on the board.

2 PREPARE THE VEGETABLES AND COOK THE STEW

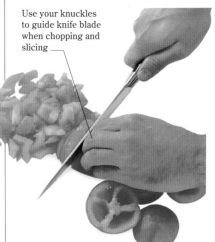

Use your knuckles to guide knife blade when chopping and slicing

1 Core the tomatoes and score an "x" on the base of each. Immerse in boiling water to split the skins, 8–15 seconds. Transfer to cold water. Peel and halve them, squeeze out the seeds, then coarsely chop each half.

2 Peel the onion, leaving a little of the root attached, and halve it lengthwise. Slice each half horizontally, then vertically, towards the root, leaving the slices attached. Cut across to make dice.

Chopped sage leaves will release their flavour into stew

Pancetta is traditional flavouring in Italian stews

3 Set the flat side of the chef's knife on top of each garlic clove and strike it with your fist. Discard the skin and finely chop 5 of the garlic cloves. Reserve the remaining garlic clove.

4 Chop the rest of the sage leaves, reserving 2 sprigs for decoration. Stack half of the pancetta slices on the chopping board and thinly slice, then finely chop. Repeat with the remaining pancetta.

Marinated beef has absorbed oil and seasoning

Paper towels absorb excess marinade

5 Remove the meat from the marinade, with the slotted spoon, and transfer to a plate lined with paper towels. Pat the meat dry with more paper towels.

6 Heat half of the remaining oil in the large pan over high heat, add half of the pieces of meat, and brown them well on all sides, 3–5 minutes.

Stir meat frequently to prevent sticking

Brown meat in batches so it colours well

! TAKE CARE !
The oil should be hot enough to sear the meat and brown it well.

7 Transfer the meat to a bowl with the slotted spoon. Add the remaining oil to the pan and brown the rest of the beef in the same way.

8 Lower the heat to medium, add the chopped pancetta, and cook, stirring occasionally with the wooden spoon, until the fat is rendered (melted), 2–3 minutes.

ANNE SAYS
"Pancetta can be very salty, therefore the stew may not need any salt added."

Red wine adds richness and depth to stew

9 Add the chopped onion to the pan and cook, stirring, until softened, 3–5 minutes longer.

10 Return the beef to the pan with the garlic, tomatoes, bay leaves, sage, remaining black pepper, stock, and red wine.

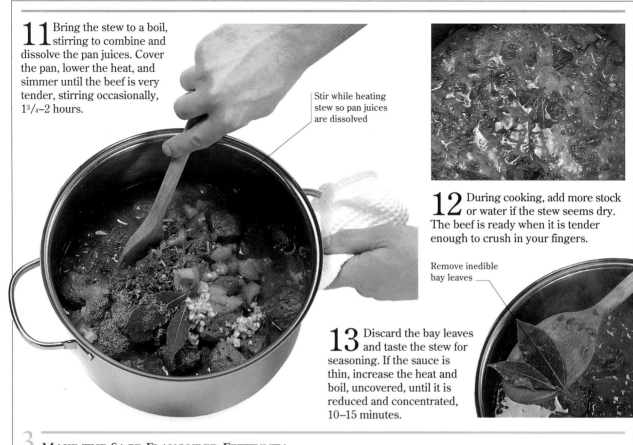

11 Bring the stew to a boil, stirring to combine and dissolve the pan juices. Cover the pan, lower the heat, and simmer until the beef is very tender, stirring occasionally, 1³/₄–2 hours.

Stir while heating stew so pan juices are dissolved

12 During cooking, add more stock or water if the stew seems dry. The beef is ready when it is tender enough to crush in your fingers.

Remove inedible bay leaves

13 Discard the bay leaves and taste the stew for seasoning. If the sauce is thin, increase the heat and boil, uncovered, until it is reduced and concentrated, 10–15 minutes.

3 MAKE THE SAGE-FLAVOURED FETTUNTA

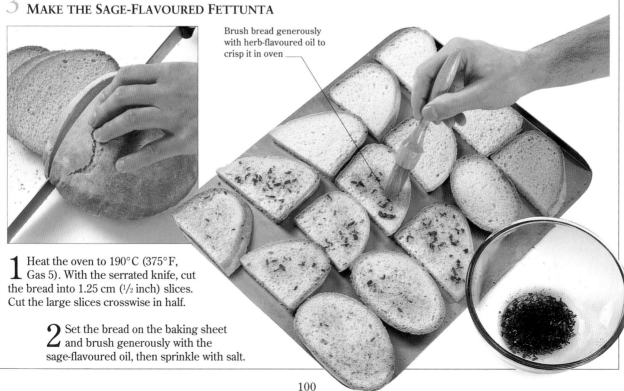

Brush bread generously with herb-flavoured oil to crisp it in oven

1 Heat the oven to 190°C (375°F, Gas 5). With the serrated knife, cut the bread into 1.25 cm (¹/₂ inch) slices. Cut the large slices crosswise in half.

2 Set the bread on the baking sheet and brush generously with the sage-flavoured oil, then sprinkle with salt.

Sage-flavoured oil permeates toasted bread

3 Bake the bread in the heated oven until toasted, 7–10 minutes. Cut the reserved garlic clove in half.

4 Rub the toasted side of each bread slice all over with the cut side of the garlic clove and transfer to the wire rack. Discard the garlic.

Beef stew is rich with favourite Tuscan flavours

Crunchy fettunta are delicious with this hearty stew

🍴 TO SERVE
Spoon the stew into a warmed serving dish and decorate with the reserved sage sprigs. Serve the sage-flavoured fettunta separately.

VARIATION

ITALIAN BEEF AND ROSEMARY STEW

In this beef stew, green olives and rosemary replace the piquant black pepper. Serve with rosemary fettunta.

1 Omit the pepper, pancetta, sage, and bay leaves. Coarsely chop the leaves from 1 large bunch of rosemary. In a large bowl, combine half with all but 45 ml (3 tbsp) of the olive oil. Reserve 60 ml (4 tbsp) rosemary-flavoured oil for the fettunta.
2 Cut the beef into cubes as directed, transfer to the large bowl and stir until well coated. Cover and marinate in the refrigerator, 8–12 hours.
3 Chop 5 garlic cloves and prepare the stew as directed, using 500 ml (16 fl oz) dry white wine instead of red, and adding the remaining rosemary in place of the bay leaves and sage.
4 Stir in the tomatoes and chopped garlic; cook until the meat is almost tender when pierced with a 2-pronged fork, 1¼–1½ hours.
5 Add 195 g (6½ oz) oil-cured green olives; cook until the meat is very tender, about 30 minutes longer. If the sauce is too thin, uncover and boil until concentrated, 10–15 minutes.
6 Meanwhile, make the fettunta as directed, with 1 garlic clove and the reserved 60 ml (4 tbsp) rosemary-flavoured oil.

SPRINGTIME VEAL STEW

Blanquette de Veau Printanière

 SERVES 6   WORK TIME 45–50 MINUTES COOKING TIME 1½–2¼ HOURS

EQUIPMENT

large flameproof casserole, with lid†

saucepan

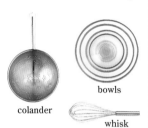

colander

bowls

whisk

2-pronged fork

large metal spoon

sieve

slotted spoon

small knife

 nutmeg grater

chef's knife

chopping board

† large saucepan can also be used

This French stew capitalizes on the paleness of veal in a creamy sauce. Fresh fennel is added for flavour, with spring carrots for a splash of colour, though they are not traditional. Nothing should brown during cooking so as to maintain the whiteness of the rich sauce. Boiled white rice is the classic accompaniment.

INGREDIENTS

boned veal shoulder†

 plain flour

lemon juice

whole clove

 onion

egg yolks

white veal stock

 butter

pickling onions

fennel

double cream

baby carrots

 nutmeg‡

bouquet garni

† 1 kg (2 lb) boned veal breast and 500 g (1 lb) boned veal shoulder can also be used for extra richness

‡ ground nutmeg can also be used

metric	SHOPPING LIST	imperial
1.5 kg	boned veal shoulder	2½ lb
1	onion	1
1	whole clove	1
1	bouquet garni, made with 5–6 parsley stalks, 2–3 sprigs of fresh thyme, and 1 bay leaf	1
	salt and white pepper	
1.5 litres	white veal stock (see box, page 124) or water, more if needed	2⅓ pints
1	large fennel bulb, weighing about 375 g (12 oz)	1
500 g	pickling onions	1 lb
500 g	baby carrots	1 lb
	For the sauce	
45 g	butter	1½ oz
30 g	plain flour	1 oz
	juice of ½ lemon	
	freshly grated nutmeg	
2	egg yolks	2
125 ml	double cream	4 fl oz

ORDER OF WORK

1 SIMMER THE VEAL

2 PREPARE THE VEGETABLES

3 MAKE THE SAUCE AND FINISH THE BLANQUETTE

1 SIMMER THE VEAL

1 Trim off and discard any fat and sinew from the veal. Cut the meat into 5 cm (2 inch) cubes.

2 Put the veal cubes into the saucepan and cover with cold water. Bring to a boil, then reduce the heat and simmer, skimming often, 5 minutes. Drain the veal, rinse with cold water, and drain again.

3 Trim the onion and peel it with the help of the small knife. Stud the side of the onion with the clove.

4 Transfer the veal to the casserole. Add the bouquet garni, clove-studded onion, salt, and white pepper, and pour in the veal stock or water. Cover with the lid, bring to a boil, and simmer very gently, skimming occasionally, until the meat is almost tender, $^{3}/_{4}$–1 hour. Meanwhile, prepare the vegetables.

Veal stock adds flavour to blanquette but water gives whiter sauce

Herbs in bouquet garni infuse veal stew with fresh aroma

2 PREPARE THE VEGETABLES

Fennel adds pleasant anise flavour to stew

1 Trim the fennel, discarding any tough outer pieces. Cut the bulb lengthwise in half, set each half flat-side down on the chopping board, and cut across into thin slices.

2 Trim and peel the pickling onions (see box, page 104). Trim the baby carrots and scrape off the skin with the back of the small knife. Alternatively, peel and trim medium carrots, and quarter them lengthwise.

HOW TO PEEL PICKLING ONIONS

Leave a little of the stalk and root on pickling onions so that they hold together during cooking.

1 Put the pickling onions in a medium bowl. Pour over hot water to cover, and let stand, 2 minutes.

2 Remove the onions from the water, one at a time, and peel them with a small knife, leaving a little of the stalk and root attached.

3 Discard the clove-studded onion and the bouquet garni from the casserole. Add the fennel, pickling onions, and carrots to the veal, with more stock or water, if needed, so that all the vegetables and the veal are covered.

ANNE SAYS
"Vegetables and veal should be well covered with stock to ensure even cooking."

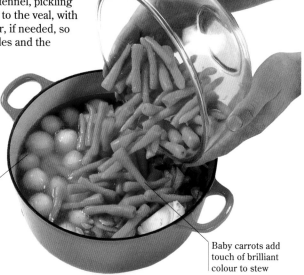

Pickling onions will remain intact during cooking

Baby carrots add touch of brilliant colour to stew

4 Cover, and continue simmering until the veal and vegetables are tender when pierced with the 2-pronged fork, 20–30 minutes.

ANNE SAYS
"If the meat is cooked before the vegetables, remove the cubes and continue simmering the vegetables."

3 MAKE THE SAUCE AND FINISH THE BLANQUETTE

1 Remove the veal and vegetables. Strain the liquid into the saucepan and simmer until well flavoured and reduced by about half, 10–20 minutes.

2 Melt the butter in the casserole. Whisk in the flour and cook until foaming, 30–60 seconds. Remove from the heat and cool slightly. Whisk in the cooking liquid and return to the heat, whisking constantly, until it boils and thickens, 3–5 minutes. Simmer until it coats the back of a spoon, 10–15 minutes.

! TAKE CARE !
If the sauce forms lumps at any stage, remove from the heat and whisk vigorously.

3 Return the veal and vegetables to the sauce and season to taste with the lemon juice, salt, white pepper, and grated nutmeg. Gently heat the blanquette so the flavours blend, 7–10 minutes longer.

ANNE SAYS
"Freshly grated nutmeg has a wonderfully aromatic flavour."

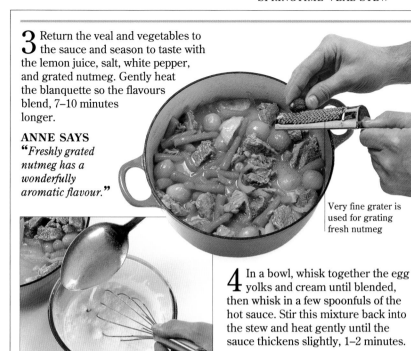

Very fine grater is used for grating fresh nutmeg

4 In a bowl, whisk together the egg yolks and cream until blended, then whisk in a few spoonfuls of the hot sauce. Stir this mixture back into the stew and heat gently until the sauce thickens slightly, 1–2 minutes.

! TAKE CARE !
Do not boil the sauce or it will curdle.

🍴 TO SERVE
Transfer the stew to a warmed serving bowl and serve immediately.

Velvety sauce is enriched with egg yolks and cream

Baby carrots and pickling onions add sweetness to veal stew

VARIATION

FRENCH WHITE VEAL STEW

In this classic version of Blanquette de Veau, *the fennel and baby carrots are replaced by mushroom caps to make a whiter stew.*

1 Omit the fennel and carrots. Cook the veal as directed.
2 Prepare the onions as directed. Wipe 250 g (8 oz) button mushrooms with damp paper towels and trim the stalks even with the caps. Cut the mushrooms into quarters if large.
3 Put the mushrooms into a small saucepan with the lemon juice, 60 ml (4 tbsp) water, salt, and pepper. Cover and cook over high heat until the liquid boils to the top of the saucepan and the mushrooms are tender, 4–5 minutes. Drain the mushrooms; reserve the liquid.
4 Cook the stew as directed, adding the mushrooms, with the onions, in place of the carrots and fennel. Stir the mushroom cooking liquid into the sauce when reducing it to a coating consistency. Finish as directed. Serve on warmed plates with boiled rice, and garnish with a fresh thyme sprig, if you like.

GETTING AHEAD
The stew can be prepared up to the addition of the egg yolks and cream, 1 day ahead, and kept, covered, in the refrigerator. Reheat the stew on top of the stove and finish the dish just before serving.

MOCK VENISON STEW

Jarret d'Agneau en Chevreuil

 SERVES 6 WORK TIME 45–50 MINUTES* COOKING TIME 2½–2¾ HOURS

EQUIPMENT

large flameproof casserole, with lid

sieve

non-metallic shallow dish

large pan

whisk

rolling pin

chef's knife

small knife

vegetable peeler

medium frying pan

wooden spoon

slotted spoon

large saucepan

ladle

2-pronged fork

bowls

paper towels

thick plastic bag

conical sieve

INGREDIENTS

lamb shanks

watercress

plain flour

celeriac

redcurrant jelly

juniper berries

shallots

vegetable oil

onions

dry red wine

butter

garlic cloves

mushrooms

carrots

red wine vinegar

black peppercorns

bouquet garni   beef stock

When lamb shanks are marinated, and then simmered in red wine with vegetables, their flavour is remarkably similar to venison. Braised red cabbage makes a colourful accompaniment.

plus 1–2 days marinating time

metric	SHOPPING LIST	imperial
6	medium lamb shanks, total weight about 1.8 kg (4 lb)	6
45 ml	vegetable oil	3 tbsp
30 g	plain flour	1 oz
750 ml	beef or brown veal stock (see box, page 109), more if needed	1¼ pints
	salt and pepper	
250 g	mushrooms	8 oz
1	celeriac, weighing about 500 g (1 lb)	1
30 g	butter	1 oz
45 ml	redcurrant jelly	3 tbsp
1	bunch of watercress for decoration	1
	For the marinade	
4	shallots	4
2	garlic cloves	2
2	onions	2
2	carrots	2
10 ml	black peppercorns	2 tsp
10 ml	juniper berries	2 tsp
1	bouquet garni, made with 5–6 parsley stalks, 2–3 sprigs of fresh thyme, and 1 bay leaf	1
30 ml	red wine vinegar	2 tbsp
750 ml	dry red wine (1 bottle)	1¼ pints

ORDER OF WORK

1 MARINATE THE MEAT

2 ASSEMBLE AND COOK THE STEW

3 FINISH THE SAUCE

106

1 MARINATE THE MEAT

1 Peel the shallots and separate into sections, if necessary. Cut each into 2–3 pieces. Set the flat side of the chef's knife on top of each garlic clove and strike it with your fist. Discard the skin.

Leave crushed garlic cloves whole for marinating

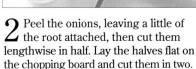

2 Peel the onions, leaving a little of the root attached, then cut them lengthwise in half. Lay the halves flat on the chopping board and cut them in two.

3 Peel the carrots, using the vegetable peeler, and trim the ends. Cut the carrots crosswise into 1.25 cm (½ inch) slices.

Use full-bodied red wine for marinating

4 Combine the black peppercorns and juniper berries in the plastic bag. Holding the end of the bag closed, crush them using the rolling pin.

ANNE SAYS
"Crushing the peppercorns and juniper berries before adding them to the marinade releases more flavour."

5 In the saucepan, combine the shallots, garlic, onions, carrots, peppercorns, juniper berries, bouquet garni, and red wine vinegar. Pour in the red wine, bring to a boil, and simmer, about 2 minutes. Transfer the marinade and vegetables to the shallow dish and set aside to cool.

6 With the chef's knife, trim off and discard any excess fat and sinew from the lamb shanks.

7 Add the lamb shanks to the dish and stir so they are coated with the marinade. Cover and marinate in the refrigerator, turning them occasionally, 1–2 days.

! TAKE CARE !
Make sure the marinade is cold before adding the lamb shanks or the meat will turn sour.

2 ASSEMBLE AND COOK THE STEW

1 Heat the oven to 180°C (350°F, Gas 4). Transfer the lamb shanks to a plate lined with paper towels. Reserve the bouquet garni. Drain the vegetables in the sieve set over a bowl. Reserve the vegetables and marinade separately. Dry the marinated lamb shanks with paper towels.

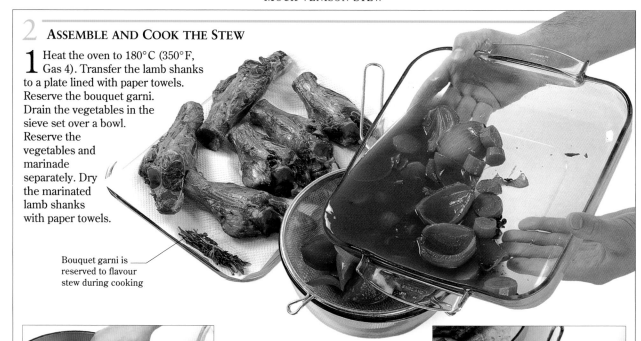

Bouquet garni is reserved to flavour stew during cooking

2 Heat half of the oil in the casserole. Add three of the lamb shanks and brown them well on all sides over high heat, 3–5 minutes.

3 Transfer the lamb to a bowl. Heat the rest of the oil and brown the remaining shanks in the same way.

Vegetables from marinade add flavour to stew

4 Add the vegetables to the casserole and cook over medium heat, stirring frequently, until they start to brown, 5–7 minutes.

5 Sprinkle the flour over the vegetables and cook, stirring with the wooden spoon, until the flour has been absorbed and the vegetables are lightly browned, 3–5 minutes.

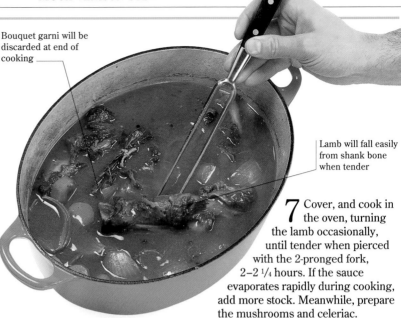

Bouquet garni will be discarded at end of cooking

Lamb will fall easily from shank bone when tender

6 Stir in the reserved marinade, scraping the bottom of the pan to dissolve the pan juices. Add the lamb shanks with any juices, the bouquet garni, beef stock, salt, and pepper.

ANNE SAYS
"*The stock should cover the meat and vegetables so add more, if necessary .*"

7 Cover, and cook in the oven, turning the lamb occasionally, until tender when pierced with the 2-pronged fork, 2–2 ¼ hours. If the sauce evaporates rapidly during cooking, add more stock. Meanwhile, prepare the mushrooms and celeriac.

BEEF OR BROWN VEAL STOCK

Stock is based on raw meat bones gently simmered with aromatic vegetables in water. Boiling should be avoided because it makes the stock cloudy. Season the stock mildly so that it does not overpower the dish to which it is added.

🍽 MAKES 2–3 LITRES (3½–5 PINTS)

🥣 WORK TIME 20–30 MINUTES

🍲 COOKING TIME 3–4 HOURS

SHOPPING LIST

1.8–2.3 kg	beef or veal bones, cut into pieces	4–5 lb
2	onions	2
2	carrots	2
2	celery sticks	2
4 litres	water, more if needed	7 pints
1	large bouquet garni	1
10	black peppercorns	10
1	garlic clove	1
5 ml	tomato purée	1 tsp

1 Heat the oven to 230°C (450°F, Gas 8). Put the bones in a roasting tin and roast until they are browned, stirring occasionally, 30–40 minutes.

2 Peel and quarter the onions and carrots. Quarter the celery. Add the vegetables to the tin and brown, stirring occasionally, 15–20 minutes.

3 Put the vegetables and bones in a stockpot. Degrease the tin. Add 500 ml (16 fl oz) water; bring to a boil. Add to the pot with the remaining ingredients and water to cover.

4 Simmer, uncovered, 4–5 hours, skimming occasionally and adding water, if necessary. Strain and boil to concentrate the flavour, if you like. Cool, and discard the fat.

8 Wipe the mushroom caps with damp paper towels and trim the stalks even with the caps, using the chef's knife. Cut the mushrooms into quarters.

Cut mushrooms into quarters for attractive presentation

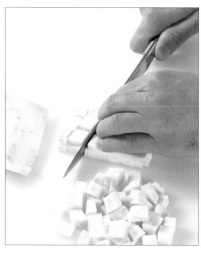

9 Peel the celeriac. Square off the sides and cut into 1.25 cm (1/2 inch) slices; stack the slices and cut into 1.25 cm (1/2 inch) strips. Cut the strips across into 1.25 cm (1/2 inch) cubes.

10 Melt the butter in the frying pan, add the celeriac, and season with salt and pepper. Cook, stirring occasionally, until tender, 8–10 minutes. Transfer to a bowl.

11 Add the mushrooms to the frying pan and cook them until all the liquid has evaporated and the mushrooms are tender, 3–5 minutes. Add to the bowl with the celeriac.

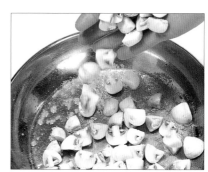

3 FINISH THE SAUCE

1 Using the 2-pronged fork, transfer the lamb shanks from the casserole to a plate and reserve them.

Sauce is rich with flavour from lamb and vegetables

2 Ladle the sauce into the conical sieve set over the large pan, pressing the vegetables with the ladle to extract all the juices.

Hold conical sieve over pan while ladling in sauce and vegetables

3 Whisk the redcurrant jelly into the sauce with plenty of pepper. Bring the sauce back to a boil and simmer until reduced by half, 20–30 minutes.

Redcurrant jelly adds touch of sweetness and colour to red wine sauce

Whisk constantly so redcurrant jelly dissolves into sauce

4 Add the mushrooms and celeriac; taste for seasoning – it should be fruity, but piquant with pepper. Return the lamb to the sauce and heat until very hot, 5–10 minutes.

¶◎¶ TO SERVE
Divide the stew among warmed plates; spoon over the sauce. Decorate with bouquets of watercress.

Red cabbage is a brilliant contrast to deep brown sauce

Marinated lamb shanks have distinct venison flavour

VARIATION
VENISON STEW WITH PEARS

Here, true venison is simmered with pears and redcurrant jelly.

1 Omit the lamb shanks. Prepare the marinade as directed. Trim the fat and sinew from 1.6 kg (3½ lb) venison stew meat and cut it into 4 cm (1½ inch) cubes. Marinate the meat and vegetables as directed.
2 Continue as directed, cooking the venison until tender, 1¼–1½ hours.
3 Meanwhile, peel 4 firm ripe pears (total weight about 625 g/1¼ lb); cut out the flower and stalk ends. Cut each pear lengthwise in half and scoop out the core. Cut each half into thirds and put them in a bowl. Sprinkle the pears with the juice of 1 lemon and toss to coat so they do not discolour.
4 Remove the venison from the sauce and set it aside. Strain the sauce into a large saucepan and whisk in the redcurrant jelly with plenty of pepper.
5 Add the pears, bring the sauce back to a boil, and simmer until tender, 6–8 minutes. Remove the pears.
6 Continue simmering the sauce until it is concentrated and has thickened slightly, 5–10 minutes. Return the venison and pears to the sauce and bring back just to a boil. Transfer to a warmed tureen.

--- **GETTING AHEAD** ---
The cooked stew can be kept, covered, in the refrigerator, 1–2 days, or it can be frozen. Reheat it on top of the stove and finish the sauce just before serving.

PERFECT PASTA AND CHEESE

🍽 SERVES 6 🥄 WORK TIME 30–35 MINUTES 🍲 BAKING TIME 25–30 MINUTES

EQUIPMENT

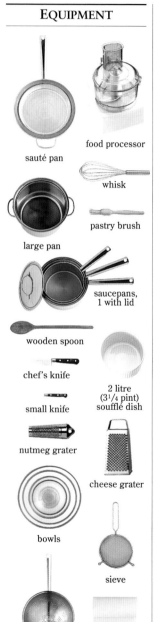

food processor

sauté pan

whisk

pastry brush

large pan

saucepans,
1 with lid

wooden spoon

chef's knife

2 litre
(3¼ pint)
soufflé dish

small knife

nutmeg grater

cheese grater

bowls

sieve

paper towels

colander

We all relate instantly to childhood favourites like macaroni cheese. In this grown-up version, quill-shaped pasta is baked in a simple cheese sauce, embellished with a mixture of sautéed wild and button mushrooms.

GETTING AHEAD
The complete dish can be prepared 1 day ahead and kept, covered, in the refrigerator. Bake just before serving.

metric	SHOPPING LIST	imperial
3	shallots	3
3	garlic cloves	3
125 g	mixed fresh wild mushrooms, such as chanterelles and shiitake	4 oz
125 g	button mushrooms	4 oz
15 ml	butter, more for soufflé dish	1 tbsp
	salt and pepper	
375 g	quill-shaped pasta	12 oz
For the topping and cheese sauce		
250 g	sharp Cheddar cheese	8 oz
1	small bunch of fresh chives	1
2	slices of white bread	2
1 litre	milk	1²/₃ pints
1	slice of onion	1
6	black peppercorns	6
1	bay leaf	1
30 g	butter	1 oz
30 ml	plain flour	2 tbsp
	freshly grated nutmeg	

INGREDIENTS

quill-shaped
pasta

wild
mushrooms

Cheddar
cheese

onion

button
mushrooms

bay leaf

shallots

milk

white bread

chives

butter

plain flour

nutmeg †

garlic
cloves

black
peppercorns

† ground nutmeg can also be used

ANNE SAYS
"If wild are not available, use all button mushrooms."

ORDER OF WORK

1 PREPARE THE
MUSHROOMS

2 PREPARE THE
TOPPING

3 MAKE THE SAUCE;
FINISH THE DISH

1 PREPARE THE MUSHROOMS

1 Peel the shallots; separate into sections, if necessary. Set them flat-side down, cut them into small dice, then finely chop them.

Discard papery skins from shallots

2 Set the flat side of the chef's knife on top of each garlic clove and strike it with your fist. Discard the skins and finely chop the garlic.

3 Wipe the wild and button mushrooms with damp paper towels. Trim the stalks, cutting the button mushroom stalks even with the caps. Slice all the mushrooms.

2 Melt 15 g (½ oz) butter in the sauté pan, add the shallots and sauté them, stirring, until soft, about 1 minute. Add the garlic, mushrooms, salt, and pepper. Continue cooking, stirring with the wooden spoon, until all the liquid has evaporated and the mushrooms are tender, 3–5 minutes.

ANNE SAYS
"I often buy a selection of different wild mushrooms for added flavour."

Variety of mushrooms makes dish more lively and colourful

2 PREPARE THE TOPPING

1 Grate the Cheddar cheese against the coarse grid of the grater. Coarsely chop the chives on the chopping board.

2 Discard the crusts from the bread slices and work to form coarse crumbs in the food processor. Combine with about one-quarter of the chives and 30 g (1 oz) of the grated cheese to form the topping.

3 MAKE THE SAUCE; FINISH THE DISH

1 Scald the milk in the saucepan with the onion slice, peppercorns, and bay leaf. Remove the pan from the heat, cover, and let the milk stand in a warm place, about 10 minutes.

2 Meanwhile, melt the butter in another saucepan over medium heat. Whisk in the flour and cook until foaming, 30–60 seconds. Remove from the heat and let cool slightly.

Freshly grated nutmeg adds aromatic flavour to sauce

3 Strain in two-thirds of the milk and whisk to mix. Discard the onion and other flavourings. Return the pan to the heat and cook, whisking constantly, until the sauce boils and thickens.

4 Grate a little fresh nutmeg into the sauce, season with salt and pepper, and simmer the sauce, about 2 minutes longer.

Coarsely grated cheese will melt into hot sauce

5 Remove the saucepan from the heat and add the remaining grated Cheddar cheese; whisk to combine thoroughly.

6 Gradually whisk in the remaining milk. Taste the sauce for seasoning and adjust as needed.

! TAKE CARE !
Do not reheat the sauce or the cheese will form strings.

PERFECT PASTA WITH THREE CHEESES

Spinach pasta is tossed with a rich sauce of French cheeses and baked in individual dishes.

7 Fill the large pan with water, bring to a boil, and add 15 ml (1 tbsp) salt. Add the quills and simmer until they are *al dente*, 5–7 minutes, or according to package directions. Stir occasionally so they do not stick. Drain the quills in the sieve, rinse under hot water, and drain again thoroughly.

8 Heat the oven to 180°C (350°F, Gas 4). Butter the soufflé dish. Return the quills to the pan. Add the cheese sauce, mushrooms, and remaining chives; stir to combine. Transfer to the soufflé dish. Sprinkle with the topping. Bake until bubbling and golden brown, 25–30 minutes.

1 Omit the Cheddar cheese, shallots, mushrooms, and chives. Trim the rind from 175 g (6 oz) Brie and 60 g (2 oz) Roquefort cheese, then cut them into 1 cm (3/8 inch) cubes. Grate 175 g (6 oz) Gruyère cheese.

2 For the parsley topping: make the breadcrumbs as directed. Chop the leaves from 1 bunch of parsley. Chop 1 garlic clove. Melt 45 g (1½ oz) butter. In a bowl, combine the breadcrumbs, butter, garlic, half of the parsley, salt, and pepper.

3 Make the cheese sauce as directed, adding all of the Brie, Roquefort, and Gruyère in place of the Cheddar. Stir in 10 ml (2 tsp) Dijon mustard and taste the sauce for seasoning, adding more mustard, if you like.

4 Cook 250 g (8 oz) spinach pasta as directed. Brush 6 individual ovenproof bowls with melted butter. Drain the pasta, rinse it, and return it to the pan. Mix in the cheese sauce and remaining parsley.

5 Spoon the pasta and cheese into the bowls and sprinkle with the topping. Bake until bubbling and golden brown, 20–25 minutes.

Golden breadcrumb and cheese crust tops pasta quills in a rich cheese sauce

¶◎¶   TO SERVE
If the top has not browned sufficiently, grill until golden, 2–3 minutes. Divide among 6 warmed plates and serve with sliced tomato salad, if you like.

Wild mushrooms with shallots and garlic update familiar macaroni cheese

ROASTED PEPPER LASAGNE WITH MUSHROOMS

🍲 SERVES 8   🥣 WORK TIME 1½ HOURS   🍲 BAKING TIME 35–45 MINUTES

EQUIPMENT

chef's knife

ladle

food processor †

small knife

wooden spoon

slotted spoon

2-pronged fork

large frying pan

pastry brush

plastic bag

bowls

23 x 32 cm
(9 x 13 inch)
baking dish

paper towels

large wide
shallow pan

tea towel

large pan

† blender can also be used

A classic dish of lasagne sheets layered with ricotta cheese, mushrooms, roasted peppers, and tomato sauce flavoured with fresh herbs. The recipe is easily doubled or tripled and freezes well.

GETTING AHEAD

The lasagne can be assembled up to 2 days ahead and kept, covered, in the refrigerator. Bake it just before serving.

metric	SHOPPING LIST	imperial
4	red peppers	4
4	green peppers	4
750 g	mushrooms	1½ lb
30 ml	olive oil, more for baking dish	2 tbsp
1 kg	ricotta cheese	2 lb
1	pinch of ground nutmeg	1
375 g	lasagne	12 oz
175 g	freshly grated Parmesan cheese	6 oz
	For the tomato sauce	
2.7 kg	plum or medium tomatoes	6 lb
6	garlic cloves	6
1	bunch of fresh basil	1
7–10	sprigs of fresh oregano	7–10
1	bunch of flat-leaf parsley	1
	salt and pepper	

INGREDIENTS

Parmesan cheese

lasagne

olive oil

ricotta cheese

green peppers

red peppers

mushrooms

fresh basil

garlic cloves

plum tomatoes ‡

flat-leaf parsley †

ground nutmeg

fresh oregano

† curly parsley can also be used

‡ two 850 g (28 oz) cans plum tomatoes can also be used

ORDER OF WORK

1. MAKE THE TOMATO SAUCE

2. MAKE THE FILLING AND COOK THE PASTA

3. FINISH THE LASAGNE

1 MAKE THE TOMATO SAUCE

1 Cut out the cores and score an "x" in the tomatoes. Immerse in boiling water to split the skins, 8–15 seconds. Transfer to cold water and peel, halve, and seed them; coarsely chop each half.

2 Set the flat side of the chef's knife on top of each garlic clove and strike it with your fist. Discard the skin and finely chop the garlic.

3 Strip the basil, oregano, and parsley leaves from the stalks. Coarsely chop the leaves with the chef's knife.

4 Put the tomatoes, half of the garlic, and two-thirds of the chopped herbs in the shallow pan. Add salt and pepper to taste. Cook the mixture over medium heat, stirring occasionally, until slightly thickened, 25–35 minutes; there should be just a little liquid left in the pan.

Deep-red ripe tomatoes give best flavour

Basil, oregano, and flat-leaf parsley are favourite Italian herbs

5 Ladle the mixture into the food processor and purée until smooth. Taste for seasoning and set aside.

2 MAKE THE FILLING AND COOK THE PASTA

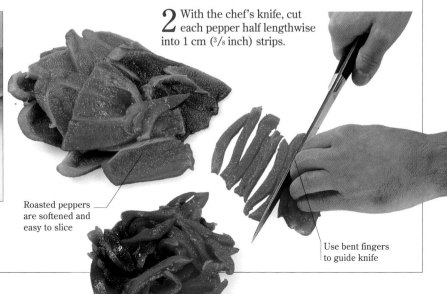

2 With the chef's knife, cut each pepper half lengthwise into 1 cm (³/₈ inch) strips.

Roasted peppers are softened and easy to slice

1 Roast and peel the peppers (see box, page 118). Cut the cores from the peppers, halve them, then scrape out the seeds.

Use bent fingers to guide knife

Trimmed mushrooms sit flat for slicing

3 Wipe the mushroom caps with damp paper towels, and trim the stalks even with the caps. Set each of the mushrooms stalk-side down on a chopping board and thinly slice them crosswise.

4 Heat the oil in the frying pan. Add the mushrooms with the remaining garlic, and salt and pepper to taste, and cook, stirring occasionally, until the liquid evaporates, 10–12 minutes.

HOW TO ROAST AND PEEL PEPPERS

Roasting peppers under the grill makes them easy to peel.

1 Heat the grill. Set the whole peppers on a rack about 10 cm (4 inches) from the heat. Grill them, turning as needed with a 2-pronged fork, until the skins are black and blistered, 10–12 minutes.

2 Put the peppers in a plastic bag, close it, and let cool so the skins are loosened by the steam.

5 Put the ricotta cheese, remaining chopped herbs, the nutmeg, salt, and pepper in a medium bowl. Stir them together until thoroughly combined.

Ricotta cheese gives filling rich creamy texture

ANNE SAYS
"If the ricotta seems dry, you can moisten it with a few spoonfuls of cream."

Chopped herbs are blended into filling mixture

3 With a small knife, peel off the skins and rinse the peppers under cold running water. Pat dry with paper towels.

6 Fill the large pan with water and bring to a boil. Add 15 ml (1 tbsp) salt and the lasagne, one sheet at a time; simmer just until tender, 8–10 minutes, or according to package directions. Using the slotted spoon, transfer the lasagne to a bowl of cold water. When cool, lift out, and drain thoroughly on the tea towel.

3 FINISH THE LASAGNE

1 Heat the oven to 180°C (350°F, Gas 4). Brush the baking dish with oil. Spread 45–60 ml (3–4 tbsp) of the tomato sauce in the dish; cover with a layer of lasagne, overlapping slightly.

2 Spread one-quarter of the ricotta mixture over the lasagne, then arrange one-quarter of the mushrooms and peppers on top. Spoon over about one-fifth of the remaining tomato sauce and one-fifth of the Parmesan.

Arrange peppers evenly over mushrooms and ricotta mixture

3 Arrange a second layer of lasagne on top and continue layering the ingredients until there are 4 layers, finishing with a fifth layer of lasagne on top. Cover with the remaining sauce and Parmesan cheese. Bake the lasagne in the heated oven until bubbling and golden brown, 35–45 minutes.

Crisp salad
complements lasagne

🍴 TO SERVE
With the chef's knife, cut the lasagne into 8 portions, and transfer them to warmed plates. Serve with lettuce and tomato salads, if you like.

Lasagne cuts into neat portions for serving

LASAGNE WITH SPINACH

Fresh spinach is featured in this lasagne, with tomato sauce, ricotta cheese, and Parmesan cheese.

1 Make the tomato sauce as directed. Omit the peppers and mushrooms.
2 Discard the tough ribs and stalks from 1 kg (2 lb) fresh spinach, then wash thoroughly. Bring a large pan of salted water to a boil. Add the spinach and simmer until tender, 1–2 minutes. Drain the spinach, rinse with cold water, and drain again. Squeeze it to remove excess water, and finely chop it.
3 Peel 2 large onions, leaving a little of the root attached, halve them lengthwise, and cut them into dice.
4 Heat 45 ml (3 tbsp) olive oil in a large frying pan. Add the onion and cook, stirring, until soft, 5–7 minutes. Add the remaining garlic, the spinach, 1 large pinch of ground nutmeg, salt, and pepper. Continue cooking, stirring occasionally, until all the liquid has evaporated, about 5 minutes. Stir in 125 ml (4 fl oz) double cream and season to taste with salt and pepper.
5 In a medium bowl, combine the ricotta cheese, remaining herbs, ground nutmeg, salt, and pepper.
6 Cook the pasta and assemble the lasagne as directed, layering the chopped spinach mixture in place of the peppers and mushrooms. Bake the lasagne as directed; serve directly from the baking dish.

AUBERGINE PARMIGIANA

 SERVES 8   WORK TIME 45–50 MINUTES*   BAKING TIME 40–50 MINUTES

EQUIPMENT

large sauté pan with lid †

bowls

large baking dish

non-metallic shallow dish

paper towels

colander

saucepan

wooden spoon

slotted spoon

chopping board

pastry brush

chef's knife

small knife

2 baking sheets

† large frying pan with lid can also be used

INGREDIENTS

aubergines

Parmesan cheese

bouquet garni

oregano

basil

sugar

tomato purée

tomatoes

garlic

mozzarella cheese

olive oil

onions

Slices of baked aubergine are the base of this parmigiana, layered with a rich tomato sauce, mozzarella, and freshly grated Parmesan cheese.

GETTING AHEAD

The parmigiana can be prepared 1–2 days ahead and kept, covered, in the refrigerator. Bring to room temperature and bake just before serving.

plus 30 minutes standing time

metric	SHOPPING LIST	imperial
4	aubergines, total weight about 1.8 kg (4 lb)	4
	salt and pepper	
175 ml	olive oil	6 fl oz
500 g	mozzarella cheese	1 lb
1	bunch of fresh basil	1
125 g	freshly grated Parmesan cheese	4 oz
	For the tomato sauce	
2.5 kg	tomatoes	5 lb
3	onions	3
5	garlic cloves	5
5–7	sprigs of fresh oregano	5–7
45 ml	tomato purée	3 tbsp
1	pinch of sugar	1
1	bouquet garni, made with 5–6 parsley stalks, 2–3 sprigs of fresh thyme, and 1 bay leaf	1

ORDER OF WORK

1 SLICE AND BAKE THE AUBERGINES

2 MAKE THE TOMATO SAUCE

3 LAYER AND BAKE THE PARMIGIANA

1 SLICE AND BAKE THE AUBERGINES

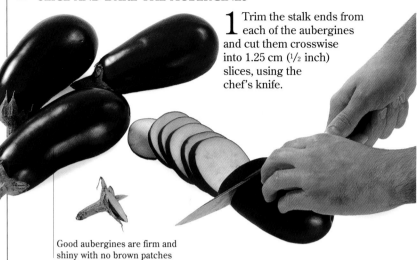

1 Trim the stalk ends from each of the aubergines and cut them crosswise into 1.25 cm (½ inch) slices, using the chef's knife.

Good aubergines are firm and shiny with no brown patches

2 Lay the slices in the shallow dish and sprinkle with salt; let stand to draw out the bitter juices, 30 minutes.

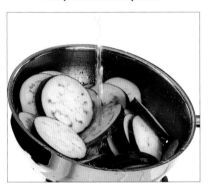

3 Heat the oven to 180°C (350°F, Gas 4). Rinse the aubergine slices well in the colander, under cold running water, to remove the salt. Dry the slices thoroughly on paper towels.

4 Oil the baking sheets. Lay the aubergine slices on the sheets and brush with oil. Bake just until tender, turning once and brushing again with oil, 20–25 minutes. Meanwhile, make the tomato sauce.

2 MAKE THE TOMATO SAUCE

1 Cut the cores from the tomatoes and score an "x" on the base of each. Immerse in boiling water until the skins start to split, 8–15 seconds. Transfer at once to cold water. When cool, peel off the skins. Cut them crosswise in half, squeeze out the seeds, then coarsely chop each half.

2 Peel the onions, leaving a little of the root attached, then cut them lengthwise in half. Lay each half cut-side down and slice horizontally, then vertically, towards the root, leaving the slices attached at the root end. Finally, cut across the onion half to make dice and chop until very fine.

Skin from crushed garlic comes off easily in your fingers

3 Set the flat side of the chef's knife on top of each garlic clove and strike it with your fist. Discard the skin and finely chop the garlic.

4 Strip the oregano leaves from the stalks and pile the leaves on the chopping board. With the chef's knife, coarsely chop the leaves.

5 Heat the remaining oil in the sauté pan, add the onions, and cook over medium heat, stirring occasionally with the wooden spoon until soft but not brown, 3–4 minutes.

Sautéed onions form base for tomato sauce

Tomatoes will cook to moist pulp in sauce so need only be roughly chopped

6 Add the chopped tomatoes to the sauté pan with the garlic, oregano, tomato purée, salt, pepper, sugar, and bouquet garni; stir to combine.

7 Cover the sauté pan and simmer the sauce over very low heat, 15 minutes. Uncover and continue cooking, stirring occasionally, until thick, about 15 minutes longer. Discard the bouquet garni and taste for seasoning.

ANNE SAYS
"*The small amount of sugar in the sauce helps cut the acidity in tomatoes.*"

3 LAYER AND BAKE THE PARMIGIANA

Mozzarella cubes will melt as parmigiana cooks

1 Cut the mozzarella into 1.25 cm (¹/₂ inch) slices. Cut the slices into 1.25 cm (¹/₂ inch) strips. Gather the strips together and cut into cubes. Strip the basil leaves from the stalks, reserving 8 sprigs for garnish. Roll up the leaves tightly and finely shred.

2 Spread about one-quarter of the tomato sauce over the bottom of the baking dish. Arrange one-third of the aubergine slices on top of the sauce in rows, overlapping them slightly.

3 Cover the aubergine slices with about one-third of the shredded basil leaves, one-quarter of the grated Parmesan cheese, and one-quarter of the mozzarella cubes.

Sprinkle mozzarella cheese evenly over aubergine slices

4 Repeat layering the tomato sauce, aubergine slices, basil, Parmesan, and mozzarella to form 3 layers. Top with the remaining tomato sauce, mozzarella, and Parmesan. Bake in the oven until bubbling and lightly browned on top, 20–25 minutes. Leave the dish to stand, 15 minutes.

🍴 TO SERVE
Cut the parmigiana into 8 portions and serve on warmed plates.

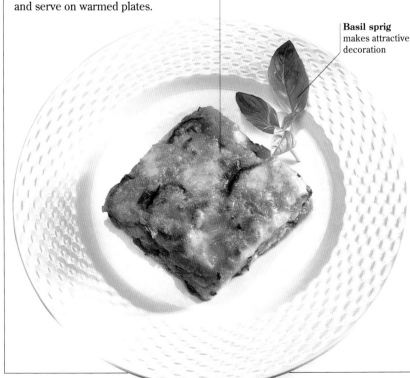

Parmesan and mozzarella cheese enrich parmigiana

Basil sprig makes attractive decoration

VARIATION

TIAN OF MEDITERRANEAN VEGETABLES

In Provence, vegetables are often baked in a traditional tian or earthenware dish.

1 Omit the tomato sauce and mozzarella. Trim and slice 6 small aubergines (total weight about 1 kg/2 lb) and 3 large courgettes (total weight about 750 g/1½ lb). Salt the slices and rinse as directed.
2 Thinly slice 6 large onions. Heat 30 ml (2 tbsp) olive oil in a large sauté pan; add the onions, salt, and pepper. Cover with foil and cook over low heat, stirring occasionally, until soft and starting to brown, 20–25 minutes.
3 Peel, seed, and chop 1.5 kg (3 lb) tomatoes. Strip the leaves from 1 bunch of fresh thyme. Cook the tomatoes and three-quarters of the thyme leaves in the pan, uncovered, as directed, about 10 minutes longer.
4 Brush eight 15 cm (6 inch) gratin dishes with oil. Spread most of the tomato mixture in each dish, reserving about 125 ml (4 fl oz). Cover with the aubergines and courgettes, alternating in a spiral pattern.
5 Sprinkle each dish with 5 ml (1 tsp) olive oil, the remaining thyme, salt, and pepper. Bake, 15–20 minutes. Add a spoonful of the reserved tomato mixture to the centre of each dish. Sprinkle with 5 ml (1 tsp) oil and 15 ml (1 tbsp) Parmesan cheese; continue baking until tender when pierced with a knife, 10–15 minutes longer.

CASSEROLES KNOW-HOW

A casserole, piping hot and straight from the oven, embodies the notion of home cooking. Whether you are serving an informal supper, or a large crowd, always use the freshest ingredients.

CHOOSING CASSEROLES

Occasion and audience are the first questions to ask when choosing a casserole. For a relaxed buffet or a party, recipes like Paella, Roasted Pepper Lasagne with Mushrooms, or Beef, Barley, and Mushroom Stew form a complete meal and are easy to serve in large quantities. The season should be taken into account, with Old Emily's Shepherd's Pie or Chicken and Beer Stew inviting in cold weather. In summer plenty of vegetables and fish are appropriate, as in Seafood and Tomato Stew or Tian of Mediterranean Vegetables. Sophisticated dishes like Five-Spice Fillet of Salmon and Tarragon Chicken would grace the grandest dinner.

GETTING AHEAD WITH CASSEROLES

A great advantage of casseroles is that they can frequently be prepared, assembled, and even cooked in advance. Many actually improve, like Turkey Mole or Prawn and Okra Gumbo. Recipes that are baked before serving, such as Aubergine Parmigiana, are ideal for preparing in advance, because all the work can be done ahead, with only the baking to be done at the last minute. Most dishes in sauce can be reheated, either in a moderate oven or on top of the stove. However, beware of sauces that can separate – cream, butter, or eggs are best added at the last minute.

Reheat using low heat to warm the food evenly and give the best results. Personally I prefer to reheat dishes in the oven, because they are less likely to scorch on the bottom of the pan. Note that flour-based sauces often thicken when they are left to stand, so they may have to be thinned with whatever liquid is appropriate.

FISH STOCK

🍽️ MAKES ABOUT 1 LITRE (1²/₃ PINTS)

🥣 WORK TIME 10–15 MINUTES

🍲 COOKING TIME 20 MINUTES

metric	SHOPPING LIST	imperial
500 g	fish bones and heads, cut into 5 cm (2 inch) pieces	1 lb
1	onion, thinly sliced	1
250 ml	dry white wine	8 fl oz
1 litre	water	1²/₃ pints
3–5	sprigs of parsley	3–5
5 ml	peppercorns	1 tsp

1 Wash the fish bones and heads; place them in a medium saucepan with the remaining ingredients.

2 Bring to a boil, and simmer, skimming occasionally with a large metal spoon, 20 minutes.

3 Strain the stock into a bowl. Cool, then cover, and keep in the refrigerator.

WHITE VEAL STOCK

🍽️ MAKES ABOUT 2–3 LITRES (3¹/₂ –5 PINTS)

🥣 WORK TIME 20–30 MINUTES

🍲 COOKING TIME 4–5 HOURS

metric	SHOPPING LIST	imperial
2 kg	veal bones, cut into pieces	4 ¹/₂lb
4 litres	water, more for blanching	7 pints
2	onions, quartered	2
2	carrots, quartered	2
2	celery sticks, quartered	2
10	peppercorns	10
1	bouquet garni	1
1	garlic clove	1

1 Put the veal bones in a large pan and cover with water. Simmer, 5 minutes, drain, and rinse well.

2 Return the bones to the pan with the remaining ingredients. Bring to a boil, skimming often, and simmer, 4–5 hours, skimming occasionally.

3 Strain the stock, and boil to concentrate the flavour, if you like. Cool, then cover, and keep in the refrigerator.

CASSEROLES AND YOUR HEALTH

By combining proteins, vegetables, and grains, casseroles help to balance your diet. If calories, cholesterol, and fat need to be considered, some casseroles can be easily modified to suit your needs. Many casseroles are either simmered or baked, so a minimum of fat is added during cooking. Some recipes are naturally low in fat. In others, the quantity of fat can be reduced or omitted altogether. When frying or sautéing, you can use olive oil or vegetable oil in place of butter. To keep cholesterol in check, the amount of meat, chicken, or fish can be reduced, and the quantity of vegetables increased. Omit rich ingredients, such as bacon, cream, and soured cream. All-vegetable recipes, like Perfect Pasta and Cheese, Roasted Pepper Lasagne with Mushrooms, and Aubergine Parmigiana, accompanied by a green salad, make a substantial vegetarian main course offering.

MICROWAVE COOKING

A microwave oven can be used to speed up the preparation of some ingredients. For example, it can help with the peeling of shallots and onions. To peel 90 g (3 oz) pickling onions or shallots, trim them and heat them in a microwave-safe bowl on High (100% power), 45 seconds. Squeeze each stalk end until the onion or shallot pops out of its skin. For tear-free onion chopping or slicing, trim the ends off the onion, then place the onion on paper towels on the microwave oven floor, and heat on High (100% power), 1 minute. Remove the skin, then slice or chop as desired.

PRESENTING CASSEROLES

I suggest many ways to present all these casseroles attractively, perhaps with garnishes of colourful herbs or twists of lemon. Some dishes are browned in the oven, a decoration in itself. A wealth of cooking dishes are available to go in the oven and take to the table, or you may prefer to transfer the food to a fresh serving dish after cooking, remembering that many have broth or a sauce and may therefore require a deep bowl. A ladle is often the appropriate serving utensil.

Many casseroles need no accompaniment and come complete with kidney beans, rice, barley, or some other carbohydrate. They may have a topping of mashed potato like French Beef and Herb Potato Pie or may be layered with pasta, like Lasagne with Spinach. Others may need an accompaniment to balance spicy flavours or a rich sauce. Unusual grains like couscous or buckwheat are a popular choice. It is hard to go wrong with a side dish of mashed potatoes, or boiled new potatoes in their skins. And simplest of all is a loaf of crusty brown or sourdough bread.

HOW-TO BOXES

In each **Creative Casseroles** *recipe you'll find pictures of all the techniques used. Some basic preparations appear in a number of recipes; these are shown in detail in "how-to" boxes:*

INDEX

ACKNOWLEDGMENTS

Photographers David Murray
Jules Selmes
Photographer's Assistant Steve Head

Chef Eric Treuille
Cookery Consultant Martha Holmberg
Home Economist Sarah Lowman

Reader Lisa Minsky

Typesetting Linda Parker
Text film by Disc to Print (UK) Limited

Production Consultant Lorraine Baird

*Anne Willan would like to thank her chief
editor Hilaire Walden, associate editor
Jackie Bobrow, and consultant editor
Cynthia Nims for their vital help with
writing this book and researching and
testing the recipes, aided by Joanna Rend
and Jane Reilly with La Varenne's chefs
and trainees.*

NOTES

- Metric and imperial measures have
  been calculated separately. Only use
  one set of measures as they are not
  exact equivalents.

- All spoon measurements are level.

- Spoon measurements are calculated
  using a standard 5 ml teaspoon and
  15 ml tablespoon to give an accurate
  measurement of small amounts.